3-Phase Lean:

Solve Any Problem
& Improve Any Process

By Damian D. Reese

For Kimberly,
who has always supported me.

2nd Edition
© February 7, 2023
Lean for Everyone

List of updates in Appendix Z

From the Author

Welcome to the 2nd edition of my book!

My commitment to Continuous Improvement led me to use the tools in this book to revise and improve on my first edition rapidly, so that it would bring you more Value. I hope you appreciate the improvements. I've outlined them all in Appendix Z, at the end of the book, which I will update each edition.

My name is Damian Reese and I'm Lean Black Belt with over 13 years of experience in process improvement. Throughout my career, I've had the opportunity to teach Lean principles to over 800 employees and executives, and I have logged over 15,000 hours of hands-on experience in Lean project and portfolio management.

I'm a Veteran of the U.S. Army, and a majority of my career was in healthcare. I now work in software development in the Salesforce ecosystem. I hold a Bachelor of Science in Business Management and a Master of Information Systems Management, which is where I was bitten by the Project Management bug that led me to my Lean Journey.

I'm thrilled to share my knowledge and experience with you through this book. I've been crafting this book for four years, and I'm confident that it will be an invaluable resource for anyone looking to improve processes and solve problems in a scientifically sound way that achieves successful results.

I believe that Lean principles should be accessible to everyone, regardless of their background or industry. That's why I started Lean for Everyone, LLC. It's also why I've created a simplified approach to process improvement that is easy to understand and implement. The approach is called 3-Phase Lean.

In this book, I will guide you through each phase of 3-Phase Lean, providing you with the tools and techniques you need to succeed.

I'm passionate about helping others achieve their goals, and I'm excited to share my knowledge and experience with you. I hope that this book will be a valuable resource for you as you embark on your own process improvement journey.

Thank you for choosing *3-Phase Lean: Solve Any Problem & Improve Any Process.*

Let's get started!

Who Should Read This Book?

The short answer is everyone.

I believe that everyone can gain enough from this book to make an important improvement in their life. Whether at work, at home, or in another organization, the tenets of Lean are valuable skills for making improvements.

Lean is for everyone. 3-Phase Lean makes it easy.

You don't have to be an industrial engineer, an executive, or even have a job to use Lean tools.

You don't have to have a certain education level, be a certain gender, or a specific age.

If you can understand the concepts of this book while reading or having it read to you, you can start making your own amazing changes.

How To Use This Book

For every reader:

This book, taken as a whole, **will seem repetitive—because it's—by design.** Every learner is different, so I give you a variety of opportunities to soak it in and use different methods to help you absorb it in your learning style.

Lean terms will be repeated several times; most are described in at least three different ways. I've also capitalized Lean terms for emphasis.

Speaking of emphasis, **I use bold to bring attention to the good stuff.** Deal with it. If you can only remember bullet points and bolded sentences, you'll be well on your way.

For the action-oriented minds:

If all you want is to get started solving problems and making improvements right now, without the fluff, you can **skip right to Chapters 5-10**. I'm serious, it's that easy and they're shorter chapters with actionable skills and tools. Go make it happen.

For the detail-oriented minds:

Chapters 1-4 are designed to give you the backstory on Lean, share some examples of Lean in action, and gently introduce Lean tools and skills. **Read straight through and when you get to Chapter 5 you'll feel confident** that Lean is full of proven methods that will add Value to your life as you implement changes. Keep going to learn how to put those tools and skills into action.

For the student minds:

I've included several resources to help you grow in your learning.

- **Questions for Students** are mostly self-reflection and action-oriented questions to help you think about applying Lean.
- **Summary and Next Steps** are to help you keep the concepts fresh in your mind.
- **Student Activity** is a section in the chapter that will prompt you to take small actions to incorporate the learning into your life.
- **Review Questions** will help you recall what the chapter highlights were.
- **3-Phase Lean Quick Guide** after Chapter 10 is a field-guide for starting to use the tools and skills.
- **Lean Terms** is a short list of important words and phrases specific to Lean, with definitions.
- **Lean Tools** is a quick reference of all the tools contained in the book.
- **Quiz Yourself** has 31 Lean quiz questions, the answers, and their explanations to help you test your knowledge.

Table of Contents

Chapter 1:
The Lean Primer

Introduction to Lean

To set the stage for this course, let's start with a story. This is one of many examples I'll share with you on your Lean Journey to help illustrate the concepts in a practical way that hopefully helps solidify your learning.

Imagine you are a chef at a busy restaurant. You are constantly receiving orders from the waitstaff, and you do your best to prepare the dishes as quickly as possible. But despite your best efforts, you find that there are always delays and bottlenecks. You are constantly having to redo dishes because they are overcooked or undercooked, and you are constantly running out of ingredients because you didn't plan ahead. It feels like no matter what you do, you can't keep up with the demand. Sound familiar?

As a chef, you are always looking for ways to improve your efficiency and effectiveness. You might try different methods for organizing your workspace, or experimenting with different cooking techniques. But despite your best efforts, it seems like there is always room for improvement. That's where Lean principles can help.

What is Lean?

The chef's scenario is a common problem in many organizations, and it's something that Lean was designed to solve. Lean is a Continuous Improvement approach that originated in the manufacturing sector but has since been applied in a wide range of industries and settings.

The goal of Lean is to identify and eliminate Waste in order to maximize Value and efficiency. In other words, Lean helps people and organizations identify and remove unnecessary steps or activities that do not add Value to the end result, and instead focus on the things that are most important to the customer or person receiving the Value the process generates.

The goal of a Lean implementation is to create a smooth and efficient workFlow that reduces unnecessary steps and costs, while also improving the quality of products and services to provide customers with more Value.

Lean Origins

You might be asking, "Where did Lean come from?" If so, this is the section for you!

Lean has its roots in post-World War II Japan, as it struggled to recover economically. After WWII, Japan was facing severe economic struggles as a result of the devastation caused by the war. The country had lost much of its infrastructure and resources, and the population was facing food shortages and poverty. In order to rebuild the economy, the government implemented policies aimed at increasing productivity and efficiency in manufacturing.

One of these policies was to focus on the production of goods that could be exported, as a way to bring in much-needed foreign currency. This led to a focus on manufacturing high-quality goods that could compete with those produced by other countries. Companies such as Toyota, who were already producing automobiles, had to find ways to increase productivity, improve quality and lower costs in order to compete in the global market.

It was in this context that Taiichi Ohno, while working as an engineer at Toyota, began to develop **the Toyota Production System (TPS)**. Ohno was a Japanese industrial engineer and businessman who is credited with developing the basis for Lean principles. He was tasked with finding ways to increase efficiency and reduce costs in the company's manufacturing processes. Ohno observed that there was a lot of Waste in the production process and that the traditional mass production methods were not working. He began to experiment with new ways of organizing the work, such as using smaller batches of parts, and involving employees in the process.

Ohno believed in the key importance of creating Value for the customer through a focus on efficiency and Continuous Improvement.

Ohno's approach was heavily influenced by the culture of Japan and the conditions of the time. The country's history of traditional craftsmanship and the need to produce high-quality goods for export, as well as the focus on efficiency and productivity to rebuild the economy, all played a role in shaping the development of TPS.

Ohno's TPS is based on the principles of respect for people and Continuous Improvement, and involves employees at all levels in the improvement process. The system emphasizes the importance of reducing Waste and increasing efficiency in order to produce high-quality goods at a low cost. TPS became the foundation of the Lean Manufacturing methodology, which is used in many industries around the world today.

Ohno implemented a number of key principles in the Toyota Production System, including Just-In-Time production, which aimed to minimize Waste by only producing what was needed when it was needed, and the use of visual controls to quickly identify problems and eliminate Waste. His approach was based on the idea that Waste could be found in every process and that it was the responsibility of all employees to identify and eliminate it. Ohno's work has had a major impact on the way that businesses around the world operate, and his ideas are still widely used today.

W. Edwards Deming, an American statistician and management consultant, played a significant role in the evolution and spread of Lean principles. Deming was invited to Japan in the 1950s to consult with Japanese companies on statistical quality control, which was an important aspect of the Toyota Production System. He taught Japanese manufacturers how to use statistical process control to improve quality, reduce variability, and increase efficiency.

Deming's teachings and methods were embraced by Toyota and other Japanese manufacturers, and they became integral to the development and spread of Lean principles. In the 1980s and 1990s, Lean principles and methods began to be adopted by companies in other industries, both in Japan and around the world.

Lean Throughout History

While Ohno and Deming are credited with formalizing the processes that make up Lean as we know it today, there are a multitude of historical examples where concepts we now know as Lean were being tested.

Lean concepts have been used by a variety of historical figures throughout history. These concepts can be found in the strategies and actions of leaders from ancient societies, as well as in the practices of modern-day industrialists and business leaders.

One historical figure who is known for implementing Lean concepts is Abraham Lincoln. During his time as President of the United States, Lincoln implemented a number of measures to **improve efficiency in the production of goods for the Union army during the Civil War**. He understood the importance of reducing Waste and increasing efficiency in order to produce goods quickly and at a low cost. He implemented measures such as standardizing production processes, using interchangeable parts, and using Visual Management tools to track progress and identify problems. These concepts are similar to those used in modern-day Lean manufacturing.

Another historical figure who is known for implementing Lean concepts is Confucius. **Confucius was a Chinese philosopher and teacher** who lived in the 5th century BCE. He believed in the importance of Continuous Improvement and emphasized the need for individuals to strive for self-improvement. Confucius believed that individuals should be constantly learning and growing, and that this process should be ongoing throughout their lives. He also believed that individuals should be held accountable for their actions and that they should take responsibility for their own development.

Sun Tzu, a Chinese general and military strategist who lived in the 4th century BCE, is another historical figure who is known for implementing Lean concepts. In his famous work **"The Art of War," Sun Tzu** emphasized the importance of strategy, planning, and efficiency in warfare. He believed that a successful military campaign required the ability to outthink and outmaneuver the enemy, rather than relying on brute force. He also believed in the importance of reducing Waste and increasing efficiency in order to achieve victory. These concepts are similar to those used in modern-day Lean thinking and are considered to be some of the earliest examples of Lean concepts in action.

Alexander the Great, a king of the ancient Greek kingdom of Macedon, is another historical figure who is known for implementing Lean concepts. Alexander was known for his military prowess and his ability to quickly conquer and control vast territories. He believed in the importance of efficiency and Waste reduction in order to achieve success. He implemented measures such as standardizing production processes, using interchangeable parts, and using Visual Management tools to track progress and identify problems.

Henry Ford, an American industrialist and business leader who lived in the 20th century, is another historical figure who is known for implementing Lean concepts. **Ford revolutionized the automobile industry** by introducing the assembly line and mass production. He believed in the importance of reducing Waste and increasing efficiency in order to produce goods quickly and at a low cost. Ford also implemented measures such as standardizing production processes, using interchangeable parts, and using Visual Management tools to track progress and identify problems. In addition, Ford paid his workers fair wages and reduced working hours, which helped to improve the standard of living for many Americans.

A modern figure who is known for implementing Lean concepts is Steve Jobs, the **co-founder of Apple Inc**. Jobs was known for his ability to identify consumer needs and to create products that meet those needs. He was also known for his ability to reduce Waste and increase efficiency in order to produce goods quickly and at a low cost. Jobs implemented measures such as standardizing production processes, using interchangeable parts, and using Visual Management tools to track progress and identify problems. He was also known for his ability to create products that were simple, elegant, and easy to use. Jobs always pushed for adding Value to his customers' lives, above all else.

One of the most well-known historical events that were successful because of Lean concepts is the Manhattan Project, which was **the U.S. government's program to develop the first atomic bomb during World War II**. The project was led by General Leslie Groves and physicist Robert Oppenheimer and involved the collaboration of several scientific and industrial organizations. The project was known for its efficient and effective use of resources, which was crucial for its success. The Manhattan Project implemented many of the principles of Lean thinking, such as reducing Waste, increasing efficiency, and using Visual Management tools to track progress and identify problems.

Another historical event that was successful because of Lean concepts is the Apollo program, which was **the U.S. government's program to send a man to the moon**. The Apollo program was led by NASA and involved the collaboration of several scientific and industrial organizations. The program was known for its efficient and effective use of resources, which was crucial for its success. The Apollo program implemented many of the principles of Lean thinking, such as reducing Waste, increasing efficiency, and using Visual Management tools to track progress and identify problems.

Another example is the **construction of the Great Wall of China**, which was built to protect the Chinese Empire from invasions by nomadic tribes. The construction of the Great Wall was a massive undertaking that required the collaboration of several engineering and construction firms. The project was known for its efficient and effective use of resources, which was crucial for its success. The construction of the Great Wall implemented many of the principles of Lean thinking, such as reducing Waste, increasing efficiency, and using Visual Management tools to track progress and identify problems.

A more modern example of an historical event that was successful because of Lean concepts is the rapid response of Toyota during **the Tsunami in 2011**, which affected the production of the company severely. The company was able to quickly and efficiently respond to the crisis by reducing Waste, increasing efficiency, and using Visual Management tools to track progress and identify problems. The company was able to quickly resume production, which helped it to minimize the impact of the crisis on its business.

A world-famous creation was successful because of Lean concepts used in **the construction of the Burj Khalifa in Dubai.** The Burj Khalifa is currently the tallest building in the world and its construction was a massive undertaking that required the collaboration of several engineering and construction firms. The project was known for its efficient and effective use of resources, which was crucial for its success. The construction of the Burj Khalifa implemented many of the principles of Lean thinking, such as reducing Waste, increasing efficiency, and using Visual Management tools to track progress and identify problems.

All of these examples demonstrate how the implementation of Lean concepts can lead to success, from small-scale improvements to large-scale projects. By reducing Waste, increasing efficiency, and using Visual Management tools to track progress and identify problems, organizations can achieve their goals more effectively and efficiently.

Lean Proliferation

As the principles of Lean were studied and applied in other industries, it became clear that Lean could be used to improve efficiency and eliminate Waste in a variety of settings, not just manufacturing. This led to the widespread adoption of Lean in various industries, including healthcare, finance, government, and service industries. Lean has also been adopted in various functions within an organization, such as supply chain management, marketing, and human resources. As more and more organizations saw the benefits of Lean, it continued to spread and evolve, leading to its widespread adoption in various industries around the world.

- **In healthcare,** Lean principles have been implemented to streamline processes and reduce wait times, resulting in improved patient satisfaction and outcomes. For example, the Virginia Mason

Medical Center in Seattle used Lean principles to reduce the time it took to complete a CT scan from an average of 45 minutes to just 15 minutes.

- **In the financial industry,** Lean principles have been applied to reduce errors, improve customer service, and streamline processes. For example, ING Direct implemented Lean principles to improve its mortgage application process, resulting in a 25% reduction in processing time and a 15% increase in customer satisfaction.
- **In the service industry,** Lean principles have been used to reduce wait times, improve efficiency, and increase customer satisfaction. For example, Walt Disney World implemented Lean principles to improve the Flow of guests through their theme parks, resulting in a 30% reduction in wait times and an increase in customer satisfaction.
- **In manufacturing,** Lean principles have been applied to reduce Waste, improve quality, and increase efficiency. For example, Toyota has used Lean principles to become one of the most efficient and successful automakers in the world.
- **In government,** Lean principles have been implemented to reduce Waste, improve efficiency, and increase transparency. For example, the U.S. Department of Veterans Affairs has used Lean principles to improve the delivery of healthcare services to veterans, resulting in a 50% reduction in wait times and an increase in patient satisfaction.

Key Lean Concepts

There are several key concepts in Lean that are helpful to understand in order to apply the approach to problem-solving or improvement:

- **Value:** Value is defined as any activity or step that is necessary to create a product or service that meets the receiver's needs or expectations. In order to identify Value, it's important to ask: "What does the receiver Value?" and if they're a customer, "What are they willing to pay for?"

- **Waste:** Waste is any activity or step that does not add Value to the product or service. There are **eight types of Waste** that are commonly identified in Lean:

  - **d**efects

  - **o**verproduction

  - **w**aiting

  - **n**ot utilizing human potential

  - **t**ransportation

  - **i**nventory storage

  - extra **m**otion

  - **e**xcess processing

  The acronym **DOWNTIME** is used to help remember the eight forms of Waste. In order to identify Waste, it's important to ask: "Is this step necessary?" and "Is there a better way to do this?"

- **Flow:** Flow is the smooth and efficient movement of materials, information, or products through a process or system. Flow is also about Value reaching the intended receiver. In order to improve Flow, it's important to identify and eliminate bottlenecks or other obstacles that prevent smooth and efficient progress.

Flow improvement focuses on **aligning resources properly** so that each person in the process can work at **single-item Flow**, which is the opposite of working with batches of work. Efficient Flow reduces Wasteful expenses like supply stockpiling, work in progress (work that has potential Value trapped while it waits), and inventory storage.

- **Bad Batching:** Another aspect of improving Flow is to reduce or eliminate bad batching. Bad batching builds unnecessary waiting into a process. One example would be waiting in the DMV to get a license renewal until 50 people total are in the batch of renewal-seekers, then the agent takes everyone's photo and makes them wait in the next batch for the next step.

- **Acceptable Batching:** There is a small level of acceptable batching when it makes sense and doesn't cause necessary delays in Value being generated for the receiver. An example is a dishwasher tray in a restaurant being completely filled with dishes before Pushing it into the dishwashing machine because Pushing each dish individually would be more Wasteful.

- **Pull:** Pull is a way of managing Flow in a Lean system, where work is only started when it's needed, rather than being Pushed through the process based on a predetermined schedule. This helps to reduce Waste by avoiding overproduction and excess inventory. Pull systems allow the receiver to Pull the Value they want from the process as they want it.

- **Push:** The opposite of a Pull System is a Push System, which Pushes the Value on its own schedule, regardless if the receiver wants or is ready to receive it. Push is a "make all we can just in case" philosophy based on approximation of the expected demand, rather than making exactly what is necessary to meet demand efficiently. As you can imagine, Push increases the risk of Waste and a mismatch to actual demand.

A Pull vs Push example is In-N-Out vs McDonald's, where cooking your food is started when you place the order vs pre-made food waiting under a heat lamp for your order to come in. In-N-Out arguably does more business than McDonald's in the same location, but produces fresher food with only slightly more wait time.

Key Principles of Lean

We already know that Lean approaches are based on the principles of Value, Waste elimination, Flow, Pull, and Continuous Improvement. Lean encourages organizations to identify what is valuable to the customer, create a continuous Flow of Value, and continuously improve processes to increase efficiency and effectiveness. By using Lean principles, organizations can increase their competitiveness, improve customer satisfaction, and achieve operational excellence.

There are several key principles that underpin the Lean approach. These include:

- **Value** is determined by those who receive it from the process

- **Value Streams** are composed of processes aligned to deliver Value to the receiver

- **Value** should Flow through the process to the receiver

- **Pull Systems** allow the receiver to Pull Value from the process as they want it
- **Lean** respects all people and encourages everyone to learn and participate
- **A culture of Continuous Improvement demonstrates respect**

Throughout this course, we'll explore these principles in more detail and see how they can be applied in various settings.

Focus on Delivering Value

In order to understand how to deliver Value to customers, it's important to first understand who the customer is and what they Value. This can be achieved through techniques such as customer interviews and surveys, as well as analyzing data on customer behavior and purchasing habits. Once the customer's needs and preferences are understood, we can identify which activities and processes add Value **from the customer's perspective**, and which do not.

What does that mean, exactly? We need to look at improving the process from the perspective of the people who receive the Value throughout the process. Value is not determined by the ones who own or touch the process. That means we ask what the intended receiver really wants from the process and try to eliminate or minimize steps that do not contribute to–or worse, impede the reception–of that Value.

The next step is to eliminate or minimize the Non-Value adding activities, also known as Waste. By identifying and eliminating Waste, resources can be focused on delivering Value to the customer. It's important to continuously seek out ways to eliminate Waste and improve processes, as customer needs and preferences can change over time.

By continuously focusing on the customer and delivering Value, an organization can improve efficiency, reduce costs, and increase customer satisfaction.

Seeking to Continuously Eliminate Waste

In the Lean methodology, one of the main goals is to continuously seek out and eliminate Waste in order to streamline processes and increase efficiency. Waste can come in many forms, such as unnecessary steps in a process, overproduction, defects, excess inventory, and unnecessary motion. **By identifying and eliminating Waste, organizations can focus their resources on creating Value for their customers.**

There are several tools and techniques that can be used to identify and eliminate Waste, such as the 5S method, which involves organizing and standardizing the workplace, and Value Stream Mapping, which involves analyzing and improving the Flow of work. **It's important to involve all employees in the process of identifying and eliminating Waste**, as they often have valuable insights and ideas on how to improve processes.

The goal of continuously seeking to eliminate Waste is to create a culture of Continuous Improvement within the organization. This requires a mindset shift from simply reacting to problems as they arise to proactively seeking out and addressing issues before they become problems. By continuously looking for ways to eliminate Waste, organizations can become more agile and responsive to changing customer needs and market conditions.

Empowering Employees to Identify and Solve Problems

In order to effectively implement Lean principles, it's important to empower employees to identify and solve problems within the organization. This means giving them the tools and resources they need to identify areas of Waste and inefficiency, as well as the authority to make changes to processes and systems. By empowering employees to take ownership of their work and continuously seek out ways to improve it, organizations can foster a culture of Continuous Improvement and drive operational excellence.

One way to empower employees to solve problems is through the use of Lean tools and techniques, such as the 5 Whys, which helps teams to identify the Root Cause of a problem. Another way is through training and development programs that teach employees how to identify and solve problems using Lean principles.

It's also important to create a supportive environment where employees feel comfortable bringing forward problems and ideas for improvement. This can be achieved through open communication channels, a culture of transparency, and a willingness to listen and act on employee feedback.

Overall, empowering employees to identify and solve problems is crucial for driving Continuous Improvement and achieving operational excellence through the use of Lean principles.

Seeking Continuous Improvement

One of the fundamental principles of Lean is the idea of Continuous Improvement, or kaizen. This means that an organization should always be looking for ways to improve its processes, products, and services in order to better meet the needs of its customers. Continuous improvement requires a culture of learning, where employees are encouraged to identify problems and propose solutions. It also requires the use of data and metrics to track progress and identify areas for improvement.

Implementing a culture of Continuous Improvement requires leadership to set the example and provide the resources and support necessary for employees to make changes. It also requires a willingness to try new ideas and to embrace change, even if it means disrupting the status quo.

There are many tools and techniques that can be used to support Continuous Improvement, such as Value Stream Mapping, Root Cause Analysis, and mistake proofing. By regularly reviewing processes and seeking ways to eliminate Waste and increase efficiency, organizations can drive ongoing improvement and stay ahead of the competition.

The Rest of the Story

In the case of our chef, Lean principles can be applied to streamline the cooking process and eliminate Waste. This might involve identifying and eliminating unnecessary steps in the cooking process, or finding ways to reduce the risk of errors such as overcooking or undercooking dishes. By applying Lean principles, the chef can improve efficiency, reduce Waste, and increase customer satisfaction.

For instance, the chef could use Kanbans and Visual Management (both concepts we'll discuss in Module 3) to improve the kitchen's efficiency by setting up a Kanban board with cards representing each dish. The waitstaff could then place an order by grabbing a card and bringing it to the chef. This would help the chef keep track of the orders and prepare them in the correct sequence. The chef could also use Visual Management techniques, such as color-coded labels or stickers, to identify ingredients that are running low and need to be restocked, items requiring special preparation, and items that need to be served together. This would help the chef plan ahead and ensure that they have the necessary ingredients on hand when they are needed. Additionally, the chef could use visual displays, such as charts or graphs, to track their progress and identify areas for improvement. This could help the chef identify bottlenecks or problems and come up with solutions to address them.

Questions for Students

Before we move on, let's pause for a moment and reflect on the story we just heard. Have you ever experienced a situation like the chef in the restaurant, where it felt like no matter what you did, you couldn't keep up with the demand? What do you think you, as the chef, before knowing anything about Lean, could have done differently to eliminate Waste and increase efficiency?

Summary and Next Steps

In this module, we introduced the concept of Lean and explored some of its key principles. In the next module, we'll delve deeper into how to identify and eliminate Waste in your organization. We'll also discuss some tools and techniques that can help you do this effectively.

Student Activity

In small groups, have students brainstorm a list of inefficiencies or areas for improvement in their current work or study environment. Have them rank the items on the list in order of impact and ease of improvement. Have them choose one item from the list to work on and come up with a plan to improve it using Lean principles.

Review Questions

1. What is the goal of Lean principles?
   - The goal of Lean principles is to eliminate Waste and create Value for customers.
2. Who is credited with developing the Toyota Production System, which forms the basis for Lean principles?
   - Taiichi Ohno is credited with developing the Toyota Production System, which forms the basis for Lean principles.
3. What is the definition of Waste in the context of Lean principles?
   - Waste in the context of Lean principles refers to any activity that does not add Value for the customer.
4. What are the eight types of Waste identified in Lean principles?
   - The eight types of Waste identified in Lean principles are defects, overproduction, waiting, not utilizing human potential, transportation, unnecessary motion, unnecessary inventory, and excessive processing. The acronym DOWNTIME can help you remember them.
5. What is the goal of Lean principles when applied to business processes?
   - The goal of Lean principles when applied to business processes is to create a smooth Flow of Value to the customer with minimal Waste.

Chapter 2:
Identifying and Eliminating Waste

Introduction to Waste

To kick off this module, let's start with another story.

Imagine you are a gardener who is responsible for maintaining a beautiful garden at a local park. One day, you notice that there is a patch of grass that is constantly overgrown and covered in weeds. You spend hours every week Pulling the weeds and trimming the grass, but no matter what you do, the weeds keep coming back. It's frustrating, because you feel like you are spending all of your time just trying to maintain the garden, instead of being able to do other things like plant new Flowers or prune the trees.

This scenario is a common example of Waste, a concept that is central to the Lean approach. Waste is any activity or process that does not add Value to the customer. In the case of the gardener, the constant weeding and trimming of the overgrown patch of grass does not add Value to the customer (in this case, the park visitors). Instead, it's just a burden on the gardener and a drain on resources.

Waste Elimination Begins With Value

Value is an important concept in Lean thinking, as it represents any activity or step that is necessary to create a product or service that meets the customer's needs or expectations. **Understanding Value is crucial for identifying and eliminating Waste, as anything that does not add Value is considered Waste.**

There are several key points to consider when thinking about Value:

1. **Value is defined by the customer:** The customer is the ultimate judge of Value, as they are the ones who will pay for the product or service. It's important to understand what the customer Values and what they are willing to pay for, and to focus on delivering those things.

2. **Value is not the same as cost:** Just because something costs a lot does not mean it adds Value. Similarly, just because something is cheap does not mean it lacks Value. It's important to understand the Value of each activity or step in relation to the customer, rather than just focusing on cost.

3. **Value can be increased through innovation:** Innovation is the process of creating new Value or finding new ways to deliver existing Value. By continuously innovating and finding new ways to add Value, organizations can increase their competitiveness and customer satisfaction.

4. **Value can be improved through Continuous Improvement:** Continuous improvement is the ongoing process of identifying and eliminating Waste in order to increase Value and efficiency. By continuously seeking out and eliminating Waste, organizations can improve the Value they deliver to customers and increase their profitability.

5. **Value must Flow throughout the entire process:** When Value Flows seamlessly, it allows for a more efficient and effective process, and ultimately leads to greater customer satisfaction and loyalty. It's also important to consider the Flow of Value in terms of time, as the Value that is delivered to the customer

must be delivered in a timely manner. This means that organizations must focus on reducing lead times and delivery times in order to increase Value for the customer.

Value is a crucial concept in Lean thinking, and is at the heart of any successful Lean Transformation. Organizations must understand the Value that their customers require and continuously strive to deliver that Value in the most efficient and effective way possible. This can be achieved through understanding the customer's needs, focusing on innovation, and continuously improving the Value Flow throughout the entire process. By considering these key points, organizations can ensure that they are delivering products or services that are truly valued by the customer.

Identifying Types of Muda Waste

Let's review the several types of Waste that can occur in organizations. These include:

- Defects: **Defects** refer to errors or rework that add no Value to the process or product. These errors can be caused by a variety of factors, such as poor quality control, lack of training, or lack of standardization. They can lead to increased costs, decreased productivity, and decreased customer satisfaction.

- Overproduction: **Overproduction** refers to the production of more than what is needed, or producing it too early. This can lead to increased costs, Wasted resources, and inventory management issues. It can also lead to delays in delivery and decreased customer satisfaction.

- Waiting: **Waiting** refers to delays in the process that add no Value. These delays can be caused by a variety of factors, such as lack of communication, lack of resources, or lack of standardization. They can lead to increased lead times, decreased productivity, and decreased customer satisfaction.

- **N**ot Utilizing Human Potential: **Not utilizing human potential** refers to holding people back from working at their full potential, either by ineffective job assignment, poor management, or lack of resources. This can lead to decreased productivity, decreased morale, and decreased customer satisfaction.

- **T**ransportation: **Transportation** refers to moving products or materials unnecessarily. This can lead to increased costs, Wasted resources, and increased lead times. It can also lead to decreased productivity and decreased customer satisfaction.

- **I**nventory: **Inventory** refers to having too much inventory, or inventory that is not being used effectively. This can lead to increased costs, Wasted resources, and inventory management issues. It can also lead to delays in delivery and decreased customer satisfaction.

- **M**otion: **Motion** refers to excessive or unnecessary movement of people or equipment. This can lead to increased costs, Wasted resources, and decreased productivity. It can also lead to decreased customer satisfaction.

- **E**xcessive Processing: **Excessive processing** refers to doing unnecessary work or using unnecessarily complex processes. This can lead to increased costs, Wasted resources, and decreased productivity. It can also lead to decreased customer satisfaction.

Formally, **these types of Waste are known in the Lean community as Muda**, which means Waste in Japanese, and refers to any activity that adds no Value to the process or product. All Muda is considered internal Waste that can be eliminated.

Mura and Muri Waste:

Two other classifications of Waste are **Mura**, and **Muri**:

- **Mura, which means unevenness or inconsistency**, refers to the fluctuations in demand and capacity that can lead to downtime. These fluctuations can be caused by a lack of standardization, poor communication, or lack of resources. When demand is greater than capacity, there can be bottlenecks in the process which can lead to downtime. When demand is less than capacity, there can be idle time and Wasted resources, leading to downtime.

  Mura is considered an external Waste that is caused by fluctuations in demand and capacity and can be improved by implementing standardized procedures and communication.

- **Muri, which means overburden or overstrain**, refers to the overwork of people, equipment, and resources. This overwork can lead to downtime, as the equipment and people may break down or become fatigued, leading to unplanned downtime. It can also lead to lower quality, increased costs, and decreased productivity.

  Muri is considered as an internal Waste since overburden on people, equipment, and resources can be improved by eliminating unnecessary work and streamlining processes.

  Tolerance of overburden is the highest form of disrespect.

Allowing overburden to persist within an organization is considered a grave disservice to the individuals and resources affected by it. It represents a disregard for their capabilities and well-being, as well as a lack of commitment to achieving optimal performance and quality. Tolerating overburden is a clear indication of a lack of respect for the individuals and resources within the organization.

Techniques for Identifying Waste

There are several techniques that can be used to identify Waste in an organization. These include:

- **Value Stream Mapping:** This is a visual representation of the Flow of materials and information through a process. It helps to identify bottlenecks, delays, and unnecessary steps.

- **Process Mapping:** This is a tool used to visually represent and analyze the steps in a process. It helps to identify bottlenecks, Waste, and opportunities for improvement. Process Maps can be created using various techniques such as Flow charts or Value Stream Maps. They can be used to understand how a process currently works and to identify areas for improvement.

- **Kaizen events:** These are focused improvement events that bring together a cross-functional team to identify and solve problems.

- **5S:** This is a system for organizing and standardizing the workplace. It involves sorting, straightening, shining, standardizing, and sustaining.

Identifying Waste by Process Mapping

Process Mapping is a tool that can be used to understand and improve a process. It involves creating a visual representation of the steps involved in a process, as well as the inputs, outputs, and any decisions that are made along the way. This can help to identify bottlenecks, delays, and unnecessary steps, and to find ways to streamline the process and increase efficiency.

Process Maps are usually created before a Kaizen event, and revised during the event. Typically, an improvement effort will have a Current State Map, which displays how the current process looks now, before the improvement, and a Future State Map, which shows how the improvement team hopes the new process to run at the end of the implementation.

In Module 8 we'll cover Process Maps as a major part of the Kaizen Event. For now, just know they're an important tool in visualizing both Value and Waste in a process.

Identifying Waste by Value Stream Mapping

Value Stream Mapping is a powerful tool for identifying Waste within an organization. It's a visual representation of the Flow of materials, information, and Value through a process. By mapping out the Current State of a process, organizations can identify areas where Waste is present and where improvements can be made.

One of the key benefits of Value Stream Mapping is that it **allows organizations to see the entire breadth of interconnected processes, from start to finish**, in one visual representation. This makes it easy to identify bottlenecks, delays, and areas of overburden. By doing so, it becomes clear where Waste is present and where improvements can be made.

Additionally, by involving employees in the mapping process, they can provide valuable insights into the process and where Waste is present, which can lead to more effective solutions. Once the Waste is identified, it can be eliminated through Continuous Improvement efforts, leading to improved efficiency and increased Value for the customer.

What's the difference between Process Mapping and Value Stream Mapping?

Simply put, a Value Stream will have many processes in it. Therefore, **a Value Stream Map will incorporate several processes at a very high level that are separately Process Mapped for greater detail**. All the processes contribute to producing Value through the Value Stream.

Figure 1: Value Stream Map Elements

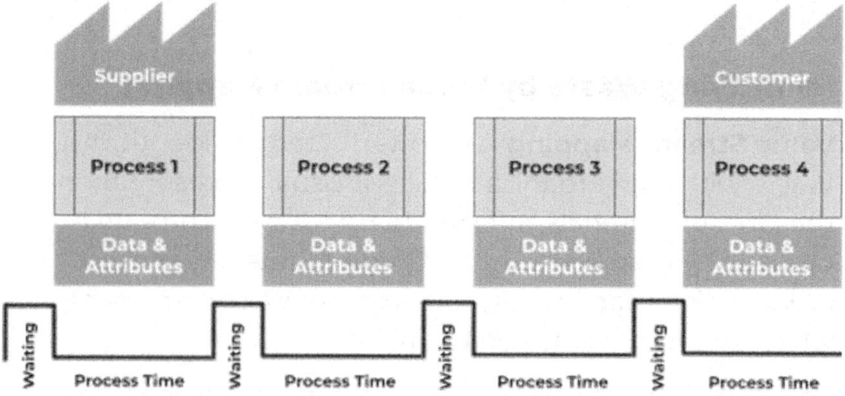

An example of a Value Stream is the lifecycle of hiring a new employee, from job opening to their first performance review. This Value Stream has many unique Processes within it, such as posting the job, recruiting candidates, qualifying and interviewing, pre-hire paperwork, onboarding, and 90-day review period. All of these individual processes are part of a Value Stream Map at a high level of detail, but each one should be Process Mapped in the most granular detail in order to begin improvement work.

The Value Stream Map is a place for understanding the overall Flow of Value, including if one process is causing Waste or waiting that impacts any of the upline or downline processes. This map also documents communication and information channels (and breakdowns), as well as the Cycle Time of each process and the wait times or delays in and between processes. **Process Maps focus solely on the steps, communication, and information in one part of the Value Stream that is being improved.**

5S for Eliminating Waste

5S is a Lean methodology for organizing and maintaining a clean, efficient, and safe work environment. It's a systematic approach to improving efficiency, productivity, and quality by eliminating Waste and standardizing work processes. The five "S"s stand for Sort, Set in Order, Shine, Standardize, and Sustain.

1. **Sort:** This step involves sorting through all the tools, equipment, and materials in the work area and keeping only what is necessary for the current and future work. Everything else should be removed and disposed of or stored in a designated area. This helps to eliminate clutter and unnecessary items that can create confusion and Waste.

2. **Set in Order:** This step involves organizing and labeling everything in the work area so that it's easy to find and use. This includes designating specific locations for tools, equipment, and materials, and

clearly marking them with labels or other visual cues. This helps to improve efficiency by reducing the time spent searching for things.

3. **Shine:** This step involves cleaning and maintaining the work area on a regular basis. This includes cleaning equipment, tools, and surfaces, and inspecting for any defects or maintenance needs. A clean and well-maintained work area is important for safety, quality, and morale.

4. **Standardize:** This step involves creating and documenting Standard Work procedures for all the activities in the work area. This includes specifying the tools, equipment, and materials that should be used, and the steps that should be followed to complete the work. Standardizing work processes helps to improve efficiency, quality, and consistency.

5. **Sustain:** This step involves maintaining the improvements made during the previous steps and continuously reviewing and improving the work processes. This includes regularly reviewing and updating Standard Work procedures, and involving all team members in Continuous Improvement efforts. Sustaining the improvements made through 5S helps to ensure that they become a permanent part of the work culture.

By following the 5S methodology, organizations can create a more efficient, productive, and safe work environment that supports Continuous Improvement.

Samantha's 5S Success

Samantha is an office manager at a small accounting firm. She has been feeling overwhelmed and disorganized with all of the paperwork and tasks she has to complete on a daily basis. She has heard about the 5S method and decides to give it a try to see if it can help her improve her work life.

- The first step of 5S is sorting, so Samantha takes a good look at her desk and office space. She finds that she has a lot of unnecessary items taking up space, such as old documents and broken office supplies. She gets rid of these items and only keeps the essentials.

- Next, she moves on to straightening. She organizes her desk and office space so that everything has a designated place. She also labels all of her drawers and shelves to make it easier to find things.

- Shining is the third step, so Samantha takes the time to clean and maintain her office space. She dusts, wipes down surfaces, and organizes her desk so that it's clutter-free.

- The fourth step is standardizing, so Samantha creates a set of procedures for maintaining her office space. She creates a schedule for cleaning and organizing, and she also creates a checklist for herself to make sure she stays on track.

- Finally, she moves on to sustaining. She makes a commitment to herself to follow her new procedures and habits every day, and she also makes sure to involve her coworkers in the process.

By implementing the 5S method, Samantha is able to significantly improve her work life and increase her productivity.

Taking It Home

Samantha was so impressed with the improvements she experienced by applying 5S at work, she decided to try using those same 5S principles in her personal life. Samantha was feeling overwhelmed and stressed out by the cluttered state of her home. She decided to try using the 5S principles to organize and streamline her living space.

- First, she sorted through all of her possessions and got rid of anything that she no longer needed or used. This helped her to declutter and free up space in her home.

- Next, she straightened everything that was left by organizing it into designated areas and storage solutions. She labeled everything clearly so that she could easily find what she needed.

- Then, she focused on shining by cleaning and maintaining the cleanliness of her home on a regular basis. This helped her to keep on top of the mess and maintain a more peaceful and organized living environment.

- Next, she standardized her systems by setting up routines and procedures for things like laundry, dishes, and general housekeeping. This helped her to stay on top of chores and prevent clutter from building up again.

- Finally, she made a commitment to sustain her new systems by regularly revisiting and adjusting them as needed. This helped her to maintain the organization and cleanliness of her home over time.

By using the 5S principles, Samantha was able to transform her chaotic and cluttered home into a calm and organized space. She found that the improved organization helped her to feel more relaxed and in control, and it also made it easier for her to find things and get things done.

Strategies for Eliminating Waste

Once Waste has been identified, there are several strategies that can be used to eliminate it. These include:

- **Streamlining processes:** Look for ways to simplify or eliminate unnecessary steps in a process.

- **Standardizing work:** Establish clear and consistent standards for how work is done. Standard work becomes the basis for the process once it has been improved, and the stepping-stone for continuously improving the process through subsequent evolutions.

- **Implementing Pull systems:** Instead of producing products or materials in advance, use a Pull system where production is triggered by customer demand. Pull systems allow customers to Pull Value from the process as they need it.

- **Utilizing Visual Management:** Use visual aids like equipment placemats, visual indicators of problems, process visualization cards, 5S elements, and even Kanban boards to track progress and identify problems.

- **Root Cause Analysis:** This is a systematic approach to identifying the underlying cause of a problem, rather than just addressing the symptoms. It can involve techniques such as the 5 Whys, fishbone diagrams, and Pareto charts.

We'll get into specific steps for this when we get to The Lean Toolkit in Chapter 5.

The Rest of the Story

Returning to our gardener's dilemma, one way to solve the weed problem would be to use the Lean principle of Root Cause Analysis. By using this method, you could identify the underlying cause of the weed problem and find a more permanent solution.

For example, you might discover that the patch of grass is getting more sunlight than the rest of the garden, which is causing it to grow more quickly and attract more weeds. By shading the area or planting a different type of grass that is more resistant to weeds, you could solve the problem for good.

By identifying and addressing the Root Cause of the problem, you can save time and effort in the long run, and create a more beautiful and sustainable garden.

Questions for Students

Take a moment to think about your current work or study environment. Can you identify any areas where Waste is occurring? How could you apply the techniques and strategies we discussed to eliminate that Waste?

Summary and Next Steps

In this module, we explored the concept of Waste and how it can occur in organizations. We also discussed techniques for identifying Waste and strategies for eliminating it. In the next module, we'll focus on the importance of involving employees in Continuous Improvement efforts and how to do this effectively.

Student Exercise

Identifying and Eliminating Waste

Instructions:

1. Take a piece of paper and divide it into three columns: "Process," "Waste," and "Solution."
2. Think of a process that you are currently involved in, such as completing a project or task at work or school.
3. In the "Process" column, write down the steps involved in the process.
4. In the "Waste" column, identify any areas of the process that are Wasteful, such as defects, overproduction, waiting, not utilizing human potential, transportation, inventory, motion, or excessive processing.
5. In the "Solution" column, brainstorm ways to eliminate or reduce the Waste identified in the "Waste" column.

Review Questions

1. What is Waste in the context of Lean principles?
   - Waste is any activity or process that does not add Value to the customer.
2. Who determines the Value of a product or service?
   - The customer is the ultimate judge of Value, as they are the ones who will pay for the product or service.
3. Is cost always a good indicator of Value?
   - No, just because something costs a lot does not mean it adds Value. Similarly, just because something is cheap does not mean it lacks Value. It's important to understand the Value of each activity or step in relation to the customer, rather than just focusing on cost.
4. How can organizations increase Value for customers?
   - Organizations can increase Value for customers through innovation and Continuous Improvement. Innovation is the process of creating new Value or finding new ways to deliver existing Value, while Continuous Improvement is the ongoing process of identifying and eliminating Waste in order to increase Value and efficiency.
5. What are some common types of Waste in organizations?
   - Defects, overproduction, waiting, not utilizing human potential, transportation, inventory, motion, excessive processing, and unused talent are all common types of Waste in organizations.
6. What is Value Stream Mapping and how is it used to identify Waste?

- Value Stream Mapping is a visual representation of the Flow of materials and information through a process. It helps to identify bottlenecks, delays, and unnecessary steps, which are all forms of Waste.

7. What is 5S and how is it used to identify and eliminate Waste?
   - 5S is a system for organizing and standardizing the workplace. It involves sorting, straightening, shining, standardizing, and sustaining, and is used to identify and eliminate Waste by reducing clutter and increasing efficiency.

8. What is a Kaizen event and how is it used to identify and eliminate Waste?
   - A Kaizen event is a focused improvement event that brings together a cross-functional team to identify and solve problems. It's used to identify and eliminate Waste by encouraging team members to come up with solutions to problems that are slowing down the process or adding unnecessary steps.

9. What is Root Cause Analysis and how is it used to identify and eliminate Waste?
   - Root Cause Analysis is a systematic approach to identifying the underlying cause of a problem, rather than just addressing the symptoms. It can be used to identify and eliminate Waste by finding and addressing the Root Causes of problems that are slowing down the process or adding unnecessary steps.

10. What is the purpose of Root Cause Analysis?
    - The purpose of Root Cause Analysis is to identify the Root Cause of a problem or issue in order to prevent it from occurring again.

Chapter 3:
Involving Employees in
Continuous Improvement

Introduction to Employee Involvement

To start off this module, let's look at a story about a company that was struggling with low morale and productivity. The company was a maker of high-end furniture, and the employees were skilled craftsmen who took pride in their work. However, they had grown frustrated with the constant changes in the production process, the lack of communication from management, and the long hours they were expected to work. As a result, they were starting to make mistakes, and the quality of the furniture was suffering.

This story illustrates the importance of involving employees in Continuous Improvement efforts. When employees feel like they have a voice and a stake in the success of the organization, they are more likely to be engaged, motivated, and productive. On the other hand, when employees feel disconnected and disengaged, they are more likely to make mistakes, and the quality of the work will suffer.

The Importance of Employee Involvement

Employee involvement is critical to the success of any Lean Transformation. Lean principles focus on empowering employees to identify and solve problems, and this can only be achieved if employees are actively involved in the process.

There are several reasons why employee involvement is so important:

- **Knowledge:** Employees are the ones who are closest to the work and have a wealth of knowledge about the processes and challenges they face. By involving them in the improvement process, organizations can tap into this knowledge and use it to identify problems and find solutions.

- **Ownership:** When employees are involved in the improvement process, they are more likely to take ownership of the changes and work to make them succeed. This leads to a greater sense of responsibility and accountability, which can drive long-term sustainability.

- **Engagement:** Involving employees in the improvement process can help to engage and motivate them. When employees feel that their ideas and opinions are Valued, they are more likely to be committed to the success of the organization.

- **Skills development:** Participating in improvement efforts can also help employees develop new skills and knowledge, which can lead to personal and professional growth.

Employee involvement is essential to the success of any Lean Transformation. By involving employees in the planning, execution, and recognition phases of the process, organizations can tap into their knowledge, increase their engagement and commitment, and help them develop new skills.

Techniques for Engaging Employees

So how can you involve employees in Continuous Improvement efforts? Here are a few techniques that can be effective:

- **Provide training:** Employees should be provided with the necessary training and tools to identify and solve problems. This can include Lean training, problem-solving tools, and other forms of support. As employees develop new skills and knowledge they can contribute more effectively.

- **Encourage participation:** Organizations should create a culture of Continuous Improvement, where employees are encouraged to speak up and share their ideas for improvement. This can be done through suggestion programs, problem-solving teams, and other methods.

- **Empowerment:** Empower employees to make decisions and take ownership of their work. This can create a sense of ownership and responsibility, which can lead to higher levels of engagement and motivation.

- **Teamwork:** Encourage teamwork and collaboration. This can create a sense of community and foster a culture of Continuous Improvement.

- **Encourage suggestion programs:** Set up a system for employees to submit ideas for improvement. Celebrate problems that are brought to the surface and share updates on the progress being made to solve them.

- **Recognize and reward contributions:** Recognize and reward employees for their contributions to Continuous Improvement. This can create a positive feedback loop and encourage more involvement. This can be done through recognition programs, awards, and other forms of appreciation.

- **Involve employees in problem-solving:** Encourage employees to identify problems and come up with solutions.

- **Involve them in the planning stage:** Employees should be involved in setting goals and creating the vision for the Lean Transformation. This helps to ensure that the goals are realistic and achievable, and that employees are committed to making them happen.

- **Involvement in decision-making:** Involve employees in decision-making processes, and seek their input and feedback. This can create a sense of ownership and engagement.

- **Use Visual Management tools:** Use tools like Kanban boards, effective daily huddles, and Lean project boards to involve employees in tracking progress and identifying problems.

- **Communication:** Foster a culture of open and transparent communication, and make sure employees are aware of what is happening in the organization. This can help to create a sense of trust and involvement.

Examples of Successful Employee Involvement

There are many examples of successful employee involvement programs. One well-known example is the Toyota Production System, which is based on the principle of "respect for people." Toyota involves employees at all levels in Continuous Improvement efforts, and this has helped the company achieve world-class levels of efficiency and quality.

Here are a few more real-world examples of successful employee involvement programs:

- **Nokia:** The Finnish telecommunications company has a program called "Nokia Way," which encourages employees to take an active role in Continuous Improvement. Employees are encouraged to identify problems and come up with solutions, and they are given the authority to make changes on the spot. This approach has helped Nokia reduce Waste and improve efficiency.

- **Southwest Airlines:** The airline has a program called "Employee Involvement Teams," which encourages employees to identify and solve problems. Teams are made up of employees from different departments and are given the authority to make changes. This approach has helped Southwest maintain a strong safety record and a high level of customer satisfaction.

- **Philips:** The Dutch electronics company has a program called "Six Sigma," which involves employees at all levels in Continuous Improvement efforts. Employees are trained in Six Sigma tools and techniques, and they are encouraged to identify and solve problems. This approach has helped Philips reduce defects and improve efficiency.

- **Johnson & Johnson:** The healthcare company has a program called "Work-Out," which encourages employees to identify and solve problems. Employees are given the authority to make changes, and they are encouraged to share their ideas and experiences with others. This approach has helped Johnson & Johnson improve efficiency and reduce Waste.

- **Xerox Corporation:** The technology company has a program called "Xerox Quality System" that encourages employees to identify and solve problems, and W.L. Gore & Associates, a manufacturer of high-tech materials that has a "lattice" organizational structure that empowers employees to take on new roles and responsibilities.

- **Danaher Corporation:** Another example of successful employee involvement is the implementation of hoshin kanri, or policy deployment, at the Danaher Corporation. Hoshin kanri is a planning and management system that involves employees in setting goals and developing action plans to achieve them. Danaher has used hoshin kanri to drive Continuous Improvement in its various business units, resulting in increased productivity and customer satisfaction.

- **Mortenson:** Other companies have implemented employee involvement programs with a focus on safety. For example, the construction company Mortenson has a program called "Everyone Goes Home" which encourages employees to speak up if they see a potential safety hazard. This program has contributed to a significant reduction in injury rates at the company.

Overall, the success of employee involvement programs depends on effective communication, leadership, and a culture that Values and empowers employees. By involving employees in Continuous Improvement efforts, organizations can tap into the collective knowledge and creativity of their workforce, resulting in increased efficiency, quality, and satisfaction for both the organization and its employees.

Creating a Lean Culture

A Lean Culture is one that Values Continuous Improvement and empowers employees to identify and solve problems. It's essential for the success of any Lean Transformation, as it helps to ensure that Lean principles are embraced and sustained over time.

These are a few of the steps an organization can use to create a Lean Culture and the role of leadership in driving this culture change:

- **Establishing a Lean steering committee:** The first step in implementing Lean principles is to establish a steering committee that will guide the transformation process. This committee should be composed of representatives from all levels of the organization, including executives, managers, and front-line workers. The committee's role is to provide leadership and direction for the Lean Transformation, as well as to serve as a resource for the rest of the organization.

- **Conducting a Value Stream analysis:** A Value Stream analysis is a critical step in implementing Lean principles. It involves mapping out the Current State of the organization's processes, from raw material input to finished product delivery. This helps to identify areas of Waste and inefficiency, and to develop a plan for improvement.

- **Creating a vision and roadmap:** Once the Current State has been mapped out, the next step is to create a vision for the Future State of the organization. This should include a clear and measurable goal for the Lean Transformation, as well as a roadmap for how to get there.

- **Implementing Lean principles:** Once the vision and roadmap have been established, the next step is to start implementing Lean principles throughout the organization. This may involve reorganizing workFlows, implementing new processes and systems, and training employees in Lean principles and tools.

- **Creating a Lean Culture:** The final step in implementing Lean principles is to create a Lean Culture within the organization. This involves creating a mindset of Continuous Improvement and empowering employees to identify and solve problems in their work area. It also involves establishing a system of metrics and feedback to track progress and identify areas for further improvement.

The Rest of the Story

The furniture company, from our example, realized the importance of involving employees in the Continuous Improvement efforts and took steps to involve them in the process. They began by holding regular meetings with employees to gather feedback and ideas for improvement. They also provided training and resources to empower employees to identify and solve problems. They implemented Visual Management tools to involve employees in tracking progress and identifying problems.

In addition to involving employees in the improvement process, the company also made changes to the production process to reduce frustration and increase efficiency. They streamlined the process and eliminated unnecessary steps, and implemented a system for clear communication between management and employees. They made changes to the work schedule to reduce the long hours and improve work-life balance for employees.

As a result of these efforts, employee engagement and motivation improved, and the quality of the furniture began to improve. The company also saw an increase in productivity and a reduction in mistakes. Employee retention saw an immediate boost, and they began to see higher quality candidates applying for jobs. The company's sales also increased as a result of the improved quality of the furniture, which helped to improve the bottom line.

The company continued to involve employees in the Continuous Improvement process, which helped to maintain and improve the improvements they had made. Over time, employees forgot what work was like before the Lean Culture because they had taken ownership of their business' success and the quality of their workplace. The empowerment they feel today has a direct impact on their engagement and satisfaction, which are all much higher than before.

Questions for Students

Think about your current work or study environment. How are employees involved in Continuous Improvement efforts? Are there any changes you would suggest to enhance employee involvement?

Summary and Next Steps

In this module, we explored the importance of involving employees in Continuous Improvement efforts and some techniques for doing this effectively. In the next module, we'll focus on the importance of customer Value and how to deliver it effectively.

Student Activity

In small groups, have students select a process or area in their current work or study environment to analyze using the Lean tools covered in the module (e.g. 5S, Value Stream Mapping, Root Cause Analysis). Have them use the tools to identify areas for improvement and come up with a plan to implement the improvements.

Review Questions

1. What is the importance of involving employees in Continuous Improvement efforts?

    Answer: Involving employees in Continuous Improvement efforts is important because it taps into their knowledge, increases their engagement and commitment, and helps them develop new skills. It also leads to a greater sense of responsibility and accountability, which can drive long-term sustainability.

2. Why is employee involvement critical to the success of any Lean Transformation?

   Answer: Employee involvement is critical to the success of any Lean Transformation because Lean principles focus on empowering employees to identify and solve problems. By involving employees in the process, organizations can tap into their knowledge and use it to identify problems and find solutions.

3. What are some techniques for engaging employees in Continuous Improvement efforts?

   Answer: Techniques for engaging employees in Continuous Improvement efforts include involving them in problem-solving, involving them in the planning stage, providing training, encouraging participation, recognizing and rewarding contributions, using Visual Management tools, and providing training and development opportunities.

4. How can involving employees in the planning stage help to ensure that the goals are realistic and achievable?

   Answer: Involving employees in the planning stage helps to ensure that the goals are realistic and achievable because they have a firsthand understanding of the processes and challenges they face. By getting their input and feedback on the goals and vision for the Lean Transformation, organizations can ensure that the goals are realistic and achievable, and that employees are committed to making them happen.

5. How does recognizing and rewarding employee contributions help to drive long-term sustainability?

Answer: Recognizing and rewarding employee contributions helps to drive long-term sustainability because it encourages employees to continue to identify and solve problems. It also creates a culture of Continuous Improvement where employees are encouraged to speak up and share their ideas for improvement.

6. How can Visual Management tools like Kanban boards, effective daily huddles, and Lean project boards be used to involve employees in tracking progress and identifying problems?

   Answer: Visual Management tools like Kanban boards, effective daily huddles, and Lean project boards can be used to involve employees in tracking progress and identifying problems by providing a visual representation of the process and progress, allowing them to easily spot problems and identify areas for improvement.

7. How can providing training and development opportunities help employees contribute more effectively to the improvement process?

   Answer: Providing training and development opportunities helps employees contribute more effectively to the improvement process by equipping them with the necessary skills and knowledge to identify and solve problems. It also helps them to develop new skills and knowledge, which can lead to personal and professional growth.

Chapter 4:
Delivering Customer Value

Introduction to Customer Value

To start off this module, let's look at a story about a company that was struggling to differentiate itself from its competitors. The company was a maker of high-end clothing, and they had a reputation for quality and style. However, they were facing increasing competition from cheaper, fast fashion brands, and they were struggling to keep up. They were considering cutting corners and sacrificing quality in order to stay competitive, but they knew this would ultimately harm their brand.

This story illustrates the importance of customer Value in business. In the Lean approach, customer Value is the measure of how well a product or service meets the needs and expectations of the customer. To be successful, it's crucial to understand what customers Value and to focus on delivering that Value as efficiently as possible.

Determining Customer Value

So how do you determine what customers Value? There are several techniques that can be used to do this, including:

- **Customer surveys:** Use surveys to ask customers directly what they Value and how well your product or service meets their needs.

- **Customer interviews:** Conduct one-on-one interviews with customers to get a deeper understanding of their needs and preferences.

- **Observation:** Observe customers using your product or service to see what they Value and how they use it.

- **Market research:** Conduct market research to understand trends and insights about your customer base.

The Kano Model

One key tool in understanding customer Value is the Kano Model. Developed by Japanese researcher Noriaki Kano, the **Kano Model is a framework for understanding customer needs and preferences**. It identifies three types of attributes: Minimum Requirements, Satisfiers, and Delighters.

- **Minimum Requirements** are those **basic attributes** that customers expect to be present, such as quality or durability.
- **Satisfiers** are **performance attributes** that customers expect to be present at a certain level, such as price or speed.
- **Delighters** are **excitement attributes** that customers do not expect, but that can greatly enhance their satisfaction, such as new technology or unique design.

To use the Kano Model, organizations must first identify the basic and performance attributes of their product or service. These are the minimum requirements that customers expect, and they must be met in order to be competitive. However, it's the excitement attributes of Delighters that can really set an organization apart from its competitors. These are the unique features or benefits that customers do not expect, but that can greatly enhance their satisfaction. By understanding the Kano Model, organizations can identify opportunities to innovate and create new Value for customers.

Figure 2: Kano Model Example

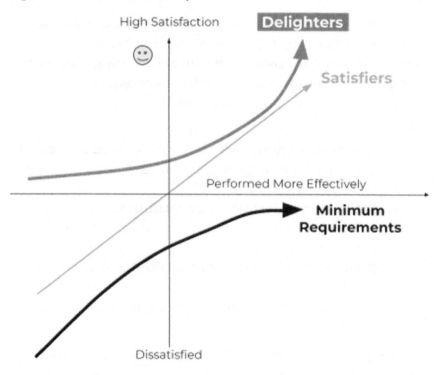

Let's look at the experience of staying at a hotel, for example. Most guests have a **Minimum Requirement** standards of a clean room, comfortable bed, and relative quiet. Guests who receive only these basics will likely be less than satisfied and look for problems to complain about.

Satisfiers are things like different kinds of pillows to choose from, complimentary toiletries that are pleasing, updated room amenities such as a big screen TV, and a location or lobby amenities that make it easy to get meals. If these performance attributes are met, guests will likely be satisfied that they had more than their basic needs met, and will feel good about paying a bit more.

Delighters would be things like delicious breakfast served free of charge each morning, receiving personal greetings and check-ins about your stay, exceptional room amenities like designer bathrooms and interesting views.

The important thing to understand about the Kano Model is that guests who receive Delighters are guests who start leaving positive reviews. Guests who only receive Minimum Requirements often write negative reviews. And guests who only experience Satisfiers will likely leave no review and their stay will be forgetful—meaning they may forget to come back in the future.

Understanding where customers find Value and where that fits on the Kano model is key to understanding where to focus improvements and where to best direct resources.

Value-Added vs Non-Value Added

Another key concept in delivering customer Value is the concept of "Value-Added" activities. These are the activities that directly contribute to the creation of Value for the customer. In contrast, "Non-Value-Added" activities are those that do not directly contribute to the creation of Value for the customer. **By identifying and eliminating Non-Value-Added activities, organizations can free up resources to focus on Value-Added activities.** This can help to improve efficiency, reduce costs, and increase customer satisfaction.

There are some Non-Value-Added activities that are necessary for compliance. They could be demanded by laws, regulations, standards, or policies. Unless the policy is able to be changed, it's often best to consider them to be "Non-Value-Added but necessary." These may not provide Value to the customer but they are necessary for the process to exist. In Lean, we try to improve these as much as possible by realigning steps and resources, but recognize that they are part and parcel to the process.

Delivering Customer Value

Once you have a good understanding of what customers Value, you can focus on delivering that Value as efficiently as possible. Here are a few strategies for doing this:

- **Focus on the most valuable features:** Don't try to be everything to everyone. Focus on the features that are most important to your customers and deliver them exceptionally well.

- **Eliminate Waste:** Use Lean tools and techniques to streamline processes and eliminate Waste, so you can deliver Value more efficiently.

- **Collaborate with customers:** Involve customers in the design and development process to ensure that you are meeting their needs and expectations.

- **Continuously improve:** Use customer feedback and data to continuously improve your product or service and stay ahead of changing customer needs.

Questions for Students

Think about a product or service that you use regularly. What do you Value most about it, and how could the company deliver that Value more efficiently?

Summary and Next Steps

In this module, we explored the concept of customer Value and how to determine and deliver it effectively. In the next module, we'll delve into some specific Lean tools and techniques that can be used to drive results in your organization.

Student Activity

In small groups, have students select a product or service that they use regularly. Have them brainstorm a list of features that they Value most about the product/service and how the company could deliver that Value more efficiently. Have them present their ideas to the class and discuss the potential impact on the customer and the business.

Review Questions

1. Why is it important to deliver Value to customers in a Lean organization?
   - It's important to deliver Value to customers in a Lean organization because customer satisfaction is a key driver of business success.
2. How can an organization identify customer needs?
   - An organization can identify customer needs through methods such as customer surveys, focus groups, and market research.
3. What is the purpose of designing processes to deliver Value efficiently?

- The purpose of designing processes to deliver Value efficiently is to minimize Waste and improve customer satisfaction.
4. What is Flow in the context of a Value Stream?
   - Flow in the context of a Value Stream refers to the smooth and efficient movement of goods or services through the Value Stream.
5. What are some strategies for creating Flow in a Value Stream?
   - Some strategies for creating Flow in a Value Stream include reducing batch sizes, eliminating Waste, and optimizing handoffs between processes.

Chapter 5:
The Lean Toolkit

Introduction to Lean Tools and Techniques

To start off this module, let's look at a story about a company that was struggling to keep up with demand. The company was a manufacturer of custom-made widgets, and they had a reputation for quality and reliability. However, they had recently landed a major contract with a new customer, and they were having trouble keeping up with the increased demand. They were falling behind schedule, and their inventory levels were fluctuating wildly. They were in danger of losing the contract, and the company's reputation was at risk.

This story illustrates how important it's to have a set of tools and techniques to help you streamline your processes and increase efficiency. In the Lean approach, there are several tools and techniques that can be used to do this.

Here are brief explanations of these tools:

- **Value Stream Mapping:** This is a visual representation of the Flow of materials and information through a process. It helps to identify bottlenecks, delays, and unnecessary steps. A Value Stream is composed of many distinct processes, and therefore many Process Maps (Module 8) could fall under one Value Stream. However, a Value Stream Map has a broader planning purpose we'll discuss in this module.

- **Kaizen:** This is the practice of Continuous Improvement, in which employees are encouraged to identify and solve problems in their work area. It's based on the idea that small, incremental improvements can add up to significant improvements over time.

- **Kaizen events:** These are focused improvement events that bring together a cross-functional team to identify and solve problems.

- **5S:** This is a system for organizing and standardizing the workplace. It involves sorting, straightening, shining, standardizing, and sustaining.

- **Visual Management:** This is a way of using visual cues to communicate important information and help people understand and improve processes. It can include things such as charts, graphs, and other visual displays.

- **Kanban:** This is a system for managing and controlling the Flow of materials through a process. It uses visual signals to indicate when work should be started and when it's ready to be moved to the next step.

- **Poka-yoke:** This is a mistake-proofing method that prevents errors from occurring in the first place. It can involve simple techniques such as using a different size or shape for different components, or more complex methods such as automated sensors.

- **Root Cause Analysis:** This is a systematic approach to identifying the underlying cause of a problem, rather than just addressing the symptoms. It can involve techniques such as the 5 Whys, fishbone diagrams, and Pareto charts.

- **Standard Work:** This is a set of standardized processes and procedures that define how work should be done.

- **Six Sigma:** This is a data-driven approach to identifying and eliminating defects in a process. It uses statistical analysis to identify the Root Cause of problems and to find solutions that are permanent and effective.

Examples of Lean Tools and Techniques in Action

To see how these tools and techniques can be applied in practice, let's look at some examples:

- **Value Stream Mapping:** A company that produces custom-made doors was having trouble keeping up with demand. They used Value Stream Mapping to identify bottlenecks in their process, and they were able to eliminate several steps that were adding no Value. As a result, they were able to significantly increase their production and delivery speed without sacrificing quality.

- **Kanban:** A company that manufactures electronics was struggling with high levels of inventory and long lead times. They implemented a Kanban system, which helped them reduce their inventory levels and improve their responsiveness to customer demand.

- **Poka-Yoke:** A food processing plant was experiencing high levels of spoilage due to expired products being used in production. They implemented a Poka-Yoke system, using sensors to automatically detect and reject expired products before they could be used. This helped them reduce spoilage and improve efficiency.

- **5S:** A company that produces custom-made furniture was having trouble with quality control. They implemented a 5S system, which helped them standardize their processes and eliminate unnecessary steps. As a result, they were able to significantly improve their quality and reduce defects.

- **Standard work:** A company that produces automotive parts was having trouble with consistency and efficiency. They implemented Standard Work procedures, which helped them ensure that work was done consistently and efficiently. As a result, they were able to reduce defects and improve delivery times.

- **Kaizen:** A healthcare organization was experiencing long wait times for patients to see a doctor. The team used the Kaizen approach to continuously improve their processes, and they were able to reduce wait times by identifying and eliminating bottlenecks in the system.

- **Kaizen Event:** A manufacturing company was experiencing high levels of Waste and defects in their production line. They conducted a Kaizen event, bringing together a cross-functional team to identify and solve the Root Causes of the problems. As a result, they were able to significantly reduce Waste and defects, leading to cost savings and increased customer satisfaction.

- **Root Cause Analysis:** A construction company was experiencing high levels of rework and delays on their projects. They used Root Cause Analysis to identify the underlying causes of the problems and implemented solutions to address them. This helped them reduce rework and improve project delivery times.

- **Visual Management:** A retail store was struggling with low employee morale and high turnover. They implemented Visual Management techniques, such as posting daily sales targets and displaying employee performance metrics, to help employees understand their role in the company's success. This helped improve morale and retention.

- **Six Sigma:** A financial services company was experiencing high levels of errors in their loan processing. They used Six Sigma methods to identify the Root Causes of the errors and implemented solutions to eliminate them. This helped them improve accuracy and customer satisfaction.

Value Stream Mapping

Value Stream Mapping is a Lean tool that is used to visually represent the Flow of materials and information through a process. It's a powerful tool for identifying Waste and improving efficiency, as it helps to highlight bottlenecks, delays, and unnecessary steps in a process.

To create a Value Stream Map, start by identifying the process or Value Stream that you want to map. This could be the process for creating a product, providing a service, or completing a task. Next, break down the process into its individual processes, and identify the Value-Added and Non-Value-Added activities. Value-added activities are those that are necessary to create Value for the customer, while Non-Value-Added activities are those that do not add Value.

Once you have identified the Value-Added and Non-Value-Added activities, you can create a visual representation of the process. This can be done using a Flowchart or other diagramming tool. Start by mapping the Current State of the process, including all of the processes and activities. Then, identify opportunities for improvement by looking for ways to eliminate Non-Value-Added activities and reduce the lead time for each step.

To make the Value Stream Map more useful, you can also include additional information such as process times, inventory levels, and throughput. This will help you to identify bottlenecks and other areas where improvements can be made.

Once you have completed the Value Stream Map, you can use it as a starting point for identifying and implementing improvements. This might involve reorganizing the process, automating certain steps, or implementing new technology. By continuously reviewing and updating the Value Stream Map, you can identify new opportunities for improvement and track your progress over time.

Value Stream Mapping is an effective tool for identifying Waste and improving efficiency, and it can be applied to a wide range of processes and industries. By visually representing the Flow of materials and information through a process, it helps to highlight areas where improvements can be made, and it provides a clear roadmap for implementing those improvements.

Kaizen Events

Kaizen events, also known as rapid improvement events or Kaizen Bursts, are focused improvement activities that bring together a cross-functional team to identify and solve problems in a short period of time, typically ranging from one to five days. The goal of a Kaizen event is to quickly identify and eliminate Waste in a process, resulting in improved efficiency and effectiveness.

There are several steps involved in conducting a Kaizen event:

1. **Identify the process or area to be improved:** The first step is to choose a process or area that is in need of improvement. This could be a specific production line, a service process, or a support function.

2. **Assemble a team:** The next step is to assemble a team of people who are familiar with the process or area being improved. This should include representatives from all relevant departments, as well as any subject matter experts who may be able to provide valuable input.

3. **Gather data:** Before the event begins, it's important to gather data about the current process or area. This can include things like process Flow diagrams, data on Cycle Times and lead times, and customer satisfaction data.

4. **Conduct the event:** During the event, the team works together to identify and eliminate Waste in the process or area. This can be done through a variety of techniques, such as Value Stream Mapping, 5S, and Root Cause Analysis.

5. **Implement improvements:** After the event, the team should implement the improvements that were identified. This may involve changes to the process, changes to the layout of the work area, or the implementation of new tools or equipment.

6. **Follow up:** It's important to follow up after the event to ensure that the improvements are sustained and that any additional issues are addressed. This may involve monitoring the process for a period of time, conducting additional Kaizen events, or implementing additional training or support.

Overall, Kaizen events are a powerful tool for identifying and eliminating Waste in a process or area. By bringing together a cross-functional team and focusing on rapid improvement, organizations can achieve significant gains in efficiency and effectiveness.

While this list of steps for a Kaizen event is relatively short, the bulk of the work is found in steps 4 and 5. We'll discuss specifics on how to facilitate this in Chapter 6: Lean for Everyone Using 3-Phase Lean.

Kanban Systems

Kanban systems are a method of inventory management that is based on the principles of Lean manufacturing. The term Kanban is derived from the Japanese word for "sign board" or "card." It's a visual system that uses cards or other visual cues to signal when inventory needs to be replenished. **Kanban systems are designed to help organizations improve the Flow of materials and reduce Waste by only producing what is needed, when it's needed.**

Kanban systems work when using a Pull system, where production is only triggered when there is a customer demand for a product. This is in contrast to a Push system, where production is based on forecasts and schedules, regardless of customer demand. Kanban systems rely on visual cues, such as cards or labels, to signal when inventory needs to be replenished. These cues are used to trigger the production process, and they are placed at key points in the production process, such as at the point of use or at the end of the production line.

Figure 3: Kanban System for Inventory

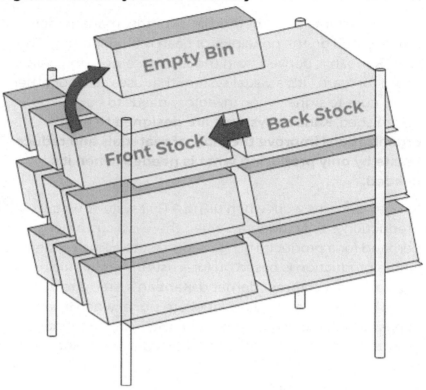

In the example supply rack above, the stock on hand is always used first and automatically replenished by the back stock when the empty bin is removed. The empty bins are placed on the top of the supply rack for refilling. Filled bins are replaced in the back of the rack.

One of the key benefits of Kanban systems is that they allow organizations to reduce inventory levels and improve inventory turnover. This is because the system only produces what is needed, when it's needed. This eliminates the need for large quantities of inventory to be held on-hand, reducing the risk of overproduction and stockouts.

Additionally, Kanban systems help to improve the Flow of materials, as they allow for just-in-time production. This means that materials are delivered to the production process just in time for them to be used, reducing the need for large quantities of raw materials to be held in inventory.

Another benefit of Kanban systems is that they are simple to implement and easy to use. **The system is based on visual cues, which are easy to understand and can be used by employees at all levels of the organization.** Additionally, Kanban systems are highly flexible, allowing organizations to adapt to changes in customer demand and production schedules. This makes it easy for organizations to respond quickly to changes in the market and improve their competitiveness.

Kanban systems are also highly scalable, making them suitable for organizations of all sizes. They can be used in a variety of industries and for a wide range of products and services. This makes **Kanban systems a versatile and cost-effective solution for inventory management.**

Kanban systems are a highly effective method of inventory management that can help organizations improve the Flow of materials, reduce inventory levels, and improve inventory turnover. By using Kanban systems, organizations can improve their competitiveness, reduce costs, and increase customer satisfaction.

Kanban systems can be found in many everyday places, such as supermarkets, fast food restaurants, and gas stations. Here are a few examples:

- **Supermarkets:** In a supermarket, a Kanban system is used to manage the inventory of products on the shelves. The store uses a card or electronic system to signal when a product is running low and needs to be restocked. This ensures that the store always has the right products in stock, without having too much inventory that can go to Waste. And if you've ever gotten a receipt with a pink or red line on the edge, you've seen a Kanban that signals the end of the paper roll is near.

- **Fast food restaurants:** Fast food restaurants use Kanban systems to manage the inventory of food items in their kitchens. This includes items such as meat, vegetables, and sauces. The system signals when items are running low and need to be restocked, ensuring that food is always fresh and available for customers.

- **Gas stations:** Gas stations use Kanban systems to manage the inventory of fuel in their tanks. The system signals when a tank is running low and needs to be refilled, ensuring that the station always has fuel available for customers.

- **Hospitals:** In hospitals, Kanban systems are used to manage the inventory of medical supplies, such as bandages, syringes, and surgical instruments. This ensures that the hospital always has the necessary supplies on hand, without having too much inventory that can expire or go to Waste.

- **Auto repair shops:** Auto repair shops use Kanban systems to manage the inventory of auto parts, such as filters, spark plugs, and brake pads. This ensures that the shop always has the necessary parts on hand to complete repairs, without having too much inventory that can go to Waste.

- **Around the house:** Some boxes of Kleenex have a Kanban included to let you know when you're nearing the end of the tissues. The last 7-10 tissues will be a different color than the rest, signaling it's time to have a replenishment ready.

Poka-yoke

While Taiichi Ohno was perfecting the Toyota Production System (TPS), Shigeo Shingo was added as a key figure in the development of TPS concepts. Shingo was a mechanical engineer who joined Toyota in 1943 and worked closely with Ohno in the late 1950s and 1960s to develop and implement the TPS. Shingo is known for his contributions to the development of the production line and the creation of the "Single Minute Exchange of Die" (SMED) system, which is a method for reducing the time it takes to change over production lines. He also developed the "poka-yoke" system, which is a method for preventing errors in manufacturing processes.

Poka-yoke, also known as mistake-proofing, is a concept from the Lean manufacturing methodology that is used to prevent errors and defects in a process. The goal of poka-yoke is to make it impossible for operators to make mistakes, or at least to make it easy to detect and correct mistakes when they do occur. This is accomplished by designing processes and equipment in such a way that errors are prevented or detected at the earliest possible stage.

One of the key principles of poka-yoke is that it's based on the idea that mistakes are a natural part of human behavior and that it's impossible to eliminate all errors completely. Therefore, the focus is on designing systems and processes that make it difficult for operators to make mistakes and that make it easy to detect and correct errors when they do occur. This can be achieved through a variety of methods, such as using visual cues and alarms, using simple and intuitive controls, and using error-proofing devices.

"Any task that requires human intervention and judgment to prevent mistakes is a mistake waiting to happen." - Shigeo Shingo

One example of poka-yoke in everyday life is the safety interlock on modern power outlets. The interlock is designed to prevent children from sticking their fingers or other objects into the outlet by only allowing a plug to be inserted when the outlet is not in use. This is a simple but effective way of preventing injury and is an example of poka-yoke in action.

Poka-yoke can also be observed in the kitchen, for example, with a gas stove. Many gas stoves have a safety valve that prevents gas from Flowing if the flame is not lit. This is a simple but effective way of preventing mistakes and accidents in the kitchen, and is an example of poka-yoke in action.

Here are some other everyday examples:

- Different shapes of plugs for different electrical power sources with different voltages.

- Tethers on gas caps that keep drivers from losing them while fueling.

It's important to note that the best poka-yoke solutions do not rely on human comprehension to be successful. Therefore, tools like color-coding, labeling, signage, and even barriers may not be enough alone to prevent mistakes from happening.

To achieve true mistake-proofing, design solutions where the easiest and most obvious way to perform a task is the safest way by removing mistake-prone methods from the equation altogether.

This highlights the fact that there are stages of poka-yoke implementations. We'll look at these in the context of dangerous railroad crossings and break them down as follows:

- **Identification:** The first step in implementing poka-yoke is to identify the problem or potential problem. In the case of railroad crossings, this would involve identifying the locations where accidents or near-misses have occurred in the past, or where there is a high risk of accidents occurring in the future.

- **Education:** Once the problem is identified, the next step is to educate the public about the dangers of railroad crossings. This could involve putting up signs or billboards with safety messages, or running public awareness campaigns to educate people about the importance of paying attention and following the rules when crossing the tracks.

- **Warning systems**: The next step is to install warning systems at the identified crossings. This could involve putting flashing lights on the signs, or installing alarms that sound when a train is approaching. The goal is to make sure that people are aware of the potential danger and have time to react before it's too late

- **Automatic barriers**: In cases where the warning systems are not enough, the next step is to install automatic barriers that drop when a train is approaching. This is a more advanced and expensive solution, but it's also one that is highly effective in preventing accidents.

- **Infrastructure improvements:** The final stage is to make infrastructure improvements to the crossings, such as building overpasses or underpasses, or even rerouting the tracks so that they no longer intersect with the roadway. This is the most expensive and time-consuming option, but it's also the most effective in preventing accidents in the long term.

These stages are not always followed in a linear fashion, but they are a good guideline to understand the process of poka-yoke and how it can be applied to different situations.

Poka-yoke is a powerful tool for preventing errors and defects in a process. It's based on the idea that mistakes are a natural part of human behavior, and that it's impossible to eliminate all errors completely. Therefore, the focus is on designing systems and processes that make it difficult for operators to make mistakes, and that make it easy to detect and correct errors when they do occur.

5S

We discussed 5S at length in Chapter 2 as a way to eliminate Waste. 5S stands for Sort, Set in Order, Shine, Standardize, and Sustain. These five steps help to create a clean, organized, and efficient work environment by eliminating unnecessary items, arranging items in a logical order, cleaning and maintaining equipment and tools, standardizing procedures and processes, and maintaining these standards over time.

5S is part of Visual Management, the concept of using visual cues to improve communication, organization, and efficiency in the workplace.

Visual Management

Visual Management is an extension of 5S and is used to improve communication and organization throughout the workplace. Visual Management tools include things like

Kanban boards, process Flow diagrams, and visual controls. These tools help to make information and processes visible to everyone in the workplace, allowing for better communication and collaboration.

Another example of Visual Management is the use of visual controls in a manufacturing facility. Visual controls are used to help workers quickly identify when a machine is in need of maintenance or when a process is not running as it should. These visual cues can be as simple as a red light that comes on when a machine is in need of maintenance, or as complex as a series of color-coded lights that indicate different stages of a process.

Together, 5S and Visual Management are powerful tools that can help to eliminate Waste, improve communication and organization, and increase efficiency in the workplace. By using these tools, organizations can create a cleaner, more organized, and more efficient work environment that leads to better products and services for customers.

Kanban Boards

Kanban boards are somewhat related to Kanban inventory systems and are used in project management, manufacturing, and logistics to help manage the Flow of materials and goods. Project management and software development use them to organize work to be completed.

A Kanban board is divided into columns that represent different stages of the production/development process, such as backlog, solutioning, in progress, quality assurance, and completed. Each column is then filled with cards or other visual cues that represent individual items or orders.

This allows team members to easily see what is happening at every stage of the process and to quickly identify and address any bottlenecks or delays.

People even make Kanban boards at home on a whiteboard with sticky notes to organize their busy lives.

Figure 4: Example of a Kanban Board

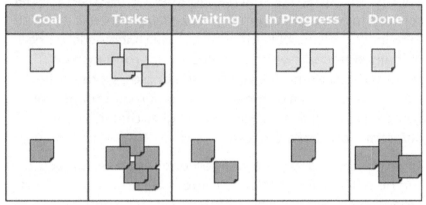

Root Cause Analysis

Lean utilizes Root Cause Analysis as a method to identify and address the underlying issues that lead to problems or inefficiencies in processes. **Root Cause Analysis is an essential tool for identifying and solving problems in a systematic and effective manner.** It's used to determine the underlying cause of a problem, rather than just addressing its symptoms.

5 Whys

One popular method for conducting Root Cause Analysis is the 5 Whys technique. This technique involves asking "why" a problem occurred, and then continuing to ask "why" in response to each answer, until the Root Cause is identified.

For example, if a problem is identified as a machine breaking down, the first "why" question would be "why did the machine break down?" The answer might be that a part was worn out. The next "why" question would then be "why was the part worn out?" The answer might be that it was not properly maintained. The next "why" question would then be "why was it not properly maintained?" The answer might be that there was no set schedule for maintenance. The final "why" question would be "why was there no schedule for maintenance?" The answer might be that there was no system in place to ensure that maintenance was performed regularly.

By asking "why" repeatedly, the Root Cause of the problem is identified. Once the Root Cause is identified, solutions can be developed to prevent the problem from recurring in the future.

A famous example is how the National Parks Service saved a national monument from excessive wear and damage. The Lincoln Memorial, one of the most iconic landmarks in the United States, was facing a problem with the discoloration and damage of its marble structure. The National Park Service, responsible for the monument's maintenance, sought to find the Root Cause of this problem through the use of the 5 Whys technique.

When they used the 5 Whys they found the Root Cause was the bright lights left on at night for security. The lights attracted insects that birds came to feast upon. The birds left droppings on the monument that were removed with powerful pressure sprayers and caustic cleansers that started damaging the marble.

By asking "Why?" enough times, the National Park Service was able to identify the Root Cause of the problem as the bright lights shining on the monument at night. This led to the solution of installing motion sensor lights, which would only turn on when someone was in the vicinity, thus reducing the amount of light shining on the monument and reducing the attraction of insects. This helped to preserve the Lincoln Memorial for future generations to enjoy.

Pro tip: if your 5 Whys lead to dead ends, backtrack until you find a branch you had missed and explore that direction. For example, if the National Park Service had asked noticed the damage with the marble and answered the first few Whys like this, they may have gotten stuck:

- Why is the marble getting damaged?
    - Because of the pressure washing and cleansers
- Why do we need to pressure wash?
    - Because of the bird droppings
- Why do we have birds?
    - Because unemptied trash cans attract them
- Why do we have trash cans?
    - Because people bring food, drinks, and other items with them to the monument

This line could have led to unsuccessful efforts like removing trash cans or imposing food and drink bans from the monument. In reality, a different path led to the real Why.

Fishbone/Ishikawa Diagram and Pareto Charts

In addition to the 5 Whys technique, other methods for conducting Root Cause Analysis include the Fishbone Diagram and the Pareto Chart. These methods are used to identify patterns and connections between different factors that may be contributing to a problem.

Fishbone diagrams, also known as Ishikawa diagrams or cause-and-effect diagrams, are used in Lean to identify the Root Cause of a problem. They are used to graphically organize and display the possible causes of a specific problem or effect. The diagram is shaped like a fish skeleton, with the problem or effect being represented at the head of the fish and the possible causes branching out from the spine.

Figure 5: Fishbone Diagram Elements

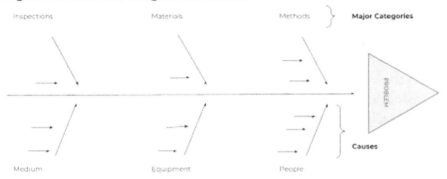

To use a fishbone diagram, first identify the problem or effect that needs to be addressed. Next, brainstorm a list of possible causes or factors that could be contributing to the problem. These causes are then organized into categories, such as people, process, equipment, materials, and environment. Each category is represented by a line branching out from the spine of the fish, and the specific causes within each category are represented by smaller branches. Once all the possible causes have been identified and organized, it's possible to identify the Root Cause of the problem by analyzing the diagram and identifying the most likely cause.

Pareto charts are another tool used in Lean to identify the Root Cause of a problem. They are used to visually represent the relative importance of different factors that are contributing to a problem. The chart is a bar graph with the factors on the horizontal axis and the frequency or quantity of the problem on the vertical axis. The bars are arranged in descending order, with the highest bar representing the most significant factor contributing to the problem. By analyzing the Pareto chart, it's possible to identify the most significant factors contributing to the problem and focus on addressing them first.

To use a Pareto chart, first identify the problem or effect that needs to be addressed. Next, gather data on the frequency or quantity of the problem for each of the contributing factors. The data is then plotted on a bar graph, with the factors on the horizontal axis and the frequency or quantity on the vertical axis. The bars are then arranged in descending order, with the highest bar representing the most significant factor contributing to the problem. By analyzing the Pareto chart, it's possible to identify the most significant factors contributing to the problem and focus on addressing them first.

Figure 6: Pareto Chart

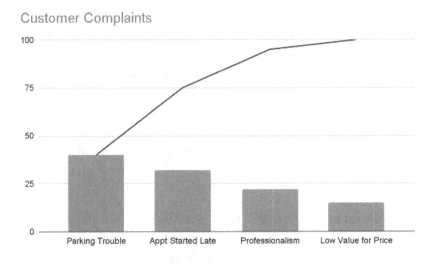

Overall, Root Cause Analysis is an essential tool in the Lean approach to problem solving and Continuous Improvement. By identifying and addressing the underlying causes of problems, organizations can improve processes, eliminate Waste, and increase efficiency and customer satisfaction.

Standard Work

Standard work is a fundamental concept in Lean methodology that **involves establishing a clear and consistent set of procedures for performing a task or process**. The purpose of Standard Work is to ensure that everyone involved in a process is using the same best practices, which leads to improved efficiency, quality, and safety.

Standard work is a key element of Continuous Improvement, as it allows organizations to identify and eliminate Waste, and to create a culture of Continuous Improvement. It's also an essential tool for creating a stable and predictable process, which makes it easier to identify and solve problems when they occur.

Standard work is not a one-time event but an ongoing process. Standard work is reviewed and updated as necessary, which takes into account changes in equipment, materials, and processes. When changes are made to the Standard Work, it's important to communicate the changes to all employees, to provide training, and to ensure that everyone understands the new procedures. The latest Standard Work becomes **the only acceptable way to perform the task** and can be used to measure process performance.

Another important aspect of Standard Work is the incorporation of Visual Management tools. These tools include things like Kanban boards, which are used to signal when a process is complete, and when new materials or resources are needed. This allows for a clear visual representation of the process, which makes it easier to identify bottlenecks and other areas of inefficiency. Visual Standard Work can consist of cards that visually display the work so that employees can grasp the Flow required to complete tasks.

Sample Standard Work:

Step #	Instructions	Notes	Time
1	Gather materials: • Clean plate • 2 slices of bread • Jar of peanut butter • Jar of jelly/jam • 2 butter knives • Paper towel	Bread slices should not be loaf heels Bread should be placed flat and separate on plate Knife should be placed on plate	1:30
2	Open both jars	Place lids outside-down on clean work surface	0:15
3	Holding the first knife securely by the handle, scoop into the peanut butter jar to load the knife with 2 oz of peanut butter		0:15
4	Changing the angle of the knife to be parallel to one slice of bread, spread the peanut butter on the large flat surface of the bread	Bread or plate may need to be stabilized with the non-spreading hand.	0:15
5	Place used knife in dirty utensils receptacle		0:05
6	Repeat step 4 with a new knife, with the jelly/jam on the unused bread		0:15
7	Place used knife in dirty utensils receptacle		0:05

8	Lift bread loaded with peanut butter by the edge to insert hand beneath bread	Use firm, gentle grasp to avoid ripping crust of bread	0:05
9	With one hand under the peanut buttered bread, touching the unbuttered side, flip the bread over and onto the exposed jelly/jam surface with a smooth, swift motion	Both pieces of bread should now be horizontal with the jelly/jam-covered slice touching the surface of the plate with un-jellied side and the unbuttered side of the peanut buttered slice face up Use careful aim to align like crust edges of the two slices of bread when laying one slice on the other to form a cohesive sandwich	0:15
10	Clean any exposed or spilled peanut butter or jelly that escaped the sandwich with paper towel before serving		0:05

Standard Work is an essential element of Lean methodology. By establishing clear and consistent procedures for performing a task or process, organizations can improve efficiency, quality, and safety. Standard work is an ongoing process that requires continuous review and improvement, and it's essential to use Visual Management tools to support the process. Implementing Standard Work is an important step towards creating a culture of Continuous Improvement.

Questions for Students

Think about your current work or study environment. Are there any Lean tools or techniques that you could apply to streamline processes and improve efficiency?

Summary and Next Steps

In this module, we explored several Lean tools and techniques that can be used to improve efficiency and streamline processes. In the next module, we'll focus on how to use data and analytics to drive Continuous Improvement.

Student Exercise

Have students create a Lean Implementation Plan for a fictional company. They should use the steps covered in the module (e.g. establish a Lean steering committee, conduct a Value Stream analysis, create a vision and roadmap) to create a detailed plan that outlines how the company can implement Lean principles and drive Continuous Improvement.

Review Questions

1. What is the role of a Lean steering committee in a Lean Transformation?
   - The role of a Lean steering committee in a Lean Transformation is to provide leadership, direction, and support for the transformation.
2. What is the purpose of conducting a Value Stream analysis?
   - The purpose of conducting a Value Stream analysis is to identify areas for improvement and Waste in a Value Stream.

3. What is the role of a vision and roadmap in a Lean Transformation?
    - The role of a vision and roadmap in a Lean Transformation is to provide a clear direction and plan for implementing Lean principles.
4. What are some strategies for implementing Lean principles in an organization?
    - Some strategies for implementing Lean principles in an organization include establishing a Lean steering committee, conducting

Chapter 6:
Lean for Everyone
Using 3-Phase Lean

Lean Improvement Approaches

There are many approaches to facilitating a Lean improvement effort, ranging from the very strict and rigid, to more flexible and approachable. Here are a few examples:

1. The **Lean Six Sigma** approach (also known as LSS) is the most widely known and complex methodology, which combines Lean principles with Six Sigma, a data-driven approach to problem-solving. It uses statistical analysis to identify and eliminate defects in a process, and focuses on Continuous Improvement.

   Six Sigma is often used in manufacturing and service industries. It's particularly effective in industries where there is a high level of complexity and variability, as it uses statistical analysis to identify the Root Causes of defects and problems. Six Sigma refers to the six standard deviations from the mean that are included in the process capability calculation.

   Six Sigma is a data-driven approach to process improvement that aims to identify and eliminate defects in a process by measuring the number of defects per million opportunities and working to reduce that number. The goal of Six Sigma is to achieve a level of quality that is effectively free of defects, or 3.4 defects per million opportunities. To achieve this level of quality, Six Sigma uses statistical analysis and a structured methodology called DMAIC (Define, Measure, Analyze, Improve, Control).

   Six Sigma Fun Facts: With 100,000 estimated airplane flights scheduled each day, a defect rate below six sigma could still allow one entire flight to crash every three days. Conversely, if Disney theme parks worldwide had a defect rate (measured as a bad experience for a guest) under six sigma, only 535 of its 157,000,000 annual visitors would have reason to complain. These examples illustrate both the power of six sigma and the magnitude required to be effective.

Some examples of industries where LSS is commonly used include healthcare, finance, and telecommunications. LSS is also used in government organizations, Non-profits, and other types of organizations. It can be applied to a wide range of processes, including those in the front office, back office, and manufacturing.

2. The **Toyota Production System (TPS)** is the original Lean approach, developed by Toyota in the 1950s. It's based on the principles of "respect for people" and Continuous Improvement, and involves employees at all levels in the improvement process.

    One famous example of TPS in action is the policy of "stop the line" in every Toyota plant. Every worker is empowered, and expected, to Pull the assembly line emergency stop cord that is in every station if they spot a defect anywhere on the automobile. Oftentimes it's something that occurred at a previous station. When the cord is Pulled, the entire line is stopped and designated responders from each area swarm to the location of the defect to immediately address it. Even the tiniest defect is extremely Valued, and the employee who finds it's honored. In this way, defects become treasures that are Valued when found, not hidden or ignored.

    An American consulting team in the 1980s once toured Japanese automotive plants to see "stop the line" in action. Upon returning to the States, they wanted to see how their American counterparts handled it. The first thing the team noticed was that the lines in the American plant rarely stopped to address a defect. The next thing they noticed was a long rumble strip of closely-spaced speed bumps that all the vehicles exiting the line drove over. When they asked what the rumble strip was for, the Americans told them it was to see if anything falls off so the vehicle could be sent to the warranty department for repair instead of being cleared for shipping.

"Stop the Line" has since been adapted in most US manufacturing plants and "Stop the Line for Safety" implemented in healthcare and other industries where human safety is at risk.

3. The **Lean Enterprise Institute (LEI)** approach is based on the principles of Lean Thinking, as outlined in the book "Lean Thinking" by James P. Womack and Daniel T. Jones. It focuses on creating Value for the customer, eliminating Waste, and continuously improving the Value Stream.

   By focusing on continuous improvement and empowering employees to identify and eliminate waste, Lean enterprises are able to increase productivity, reduce costs, and improve customer satisfaction. The LEI approach is based on the idea that Lean is not just a set of tools and techniques, but a way of thinking about business and a culture that prioritizes continuous improvement.

4. The **Lean Startup** approach is a method for developing new products or services, based on the principles of Lean Thinking. It involves rapid prototyping, customer feedback, and continuous iteration to quickly identify and deliver Value to

customers. This looks somewhat different from the improvement efforts because the goal is focused on building a 360-degree view of a single product or service while still in the planning stage, rather than solving existing problems in the Current State.

5. The **Kaizen** approach is a method for Continuous Improvement, based on the principles of small, incremental changes. It involves empowering employees to identify and solve problems, and using tools like Kaizen events and Poka-Yoke (error proofing) to eliminate Waste. This approach can seem like it blurs the lines between all the other methodologies, Pulling the best of each into a focused Kaizen Event for rapid improvement.

   Additionally, Kaizen is about empowering the entire organization, from top to bottom, to get involved in continuous improvement efforts. This approach values the involvement of all employees, regardless of their level or department, and encourages them to suggest and implement solutions to problems. By making small, incremental changes, the organization can continuously improve, create a culture of excellence, and ultimately drive business success.

6. The **3-Phase Lean** approach is specific to this book, and incorporates many of the principles of the other methodologies in this list. The tools and processes are simplified, and absent of dogma that may act as a barrier to adoption of its predecessors.

A3 Thinking and Documents

Each Lean approach follows its own methodology, but they all traditionally document on a large-format visual page called an A3.

An A3 is a structured format for documenting and analyzing a process. The term A3 just refers to the paper size, which is often known as 11x17, though the exact dimensions are 29.7 cm x 42 cm or 11.7 in x 16.5 in. No matter the method or measurement, an A3 is considered the standard documentation tool for improvement projects.

Lean Six Sigma A3s use the rigid DMAIC format (explained above). Most Lean practitioners use a 5-Box, 7-Box, or 9-Box A3. The 9-Box has become the standard in recent years because it can align to DMAIC to compare Lean and LSS outcomes. The 9-Box A3 consists of nine boxes, arranged in a 3x3 grid, that can be used to document the process and identify opportunities for improvement.

Figure 7: 9-Box A3 Format

A3 Header Info		
Reason for Action	Gap Analysis	Implementation Plan
Current State	Solution Approach	Sustainment Plan
Target State	Rapid Experiments	Project Review

Introducing: 3-Phase Lean

While the 9-Box method is highly effective, for this course I've simplified the elements of a 9-Box A3 into a method called 3-Phase Lean. The reason for this is to increase the approachability. I want every person, in every industry and every personal situation to be able to improve processes and solve problems without the headache of rigorous methodology and dogma.

Figure 8: 3-Phase Lean A3 Format

Phase 1: Cut the Clutter	Phase 2: Fix the Flow	Phase 3: Sustain the Success

3-Phase Lean is the heart of the Lean for Everyone mission.

Here's a brief overview of the 3-Phase Lean process:

- **Phase 1: Cut the Clutter**

  During this phase, the focus is on identifying and eliminating Waste in the current process. This phase starts with a thorough analysis of the Current State of the process, including identifying areas of inefficiency, delays, bottlenecks, and unnecessary steps. The key tool used in this phase is Process Mapping, which helps to visualize the steps in being performed and the Flow of materials and information throughout the process. This phase also includes implementing techniques such as Kanban to improve the Flow of materials and reduce Waste, 5S to improve workFlow, and Visual Management to bring hidden Waste to the surface.

- **Phase 2: Fix the Flow**

  This phase centers on identifying and addressing any bottlenecks or issues with the current processes that are hindering the overall performance and preventing you from achieving your goals. This phase includes analyzing data and using problem-solving tools such as Root Cause Analysis and the 5 Whys to identify the Root Cause of the problem. In this phase, the focus of the activities is on optimizing the Flow of materials and information through the process, while improving Value received from the process.

- **Phase 3: Sustain for Success**

  The final phase focuses on maintaining and continuously improving the improvements made in the previous phases. By implementing Standard Work and a Sustainment Plan, this phase helps to ensure that the improvements made are long-lasting and improve the overall performance of the organization. Sustainment also includes measuring the results and auditing processes to ensure that the improvements are being sustained and that any issues are quickly identified and addressed. This phase is crucial for ensuring that the organization is continuously improving and that the benefits of the previous phases are not lost over time..

In the next three chapters, we'll delve deeper into each phase of 3-Phase Lean, providing specific tools and techniques to help you implement these principles in your own organization.

Whether you're looking to improve efficiency in your manufacturing plant, streamline your office processes, or simply find ways to make your life run more smoothly, 3-Phase Lean is an effective and accessible method for achieving your goals. We'll cover everything from identifying Waste and optimizing Flow to maintaining and continuously improving your results. So, get ready to start your Lean Journey and achieve success in all aspects of your life and work.

Questions for Students:

1. How can your organization involve employees at all levels in the improvement process similar to the Toyota Production System?
2. Can you think of any industry where Lean Six Sigma would be particularly effective?
3. How can the Lean Startup approach be useful for your organization when developing new products or services?
4. How can you adapt "stop the line" policy in your organization? How do you think it would be beneficial?
5. How do you see the Lean approach being applied to front office and back office processes in your organization?

Summary and Next Steps:

In this module, we discussed various Lean improvement approaches, including Lean Six Sigma, the Toyota Production System, and the Lean Enterprise Institute approach. We also touched on the Lean Startup approach for developing new products or services. By understanding these different approaches, students will be able to choose the best method for their specific organization and situation. In the next module, we'll dive deeper into specific Lean tools and techniques that can be used to improve processes and increase efficiency.

Student Activity:

Write down some problems you'd like to solve or processes you'd like to improve. What Lean approach would be the best fit for each issue? Which ones would be the biggest wins? Which are likely the quickest wins? Which are the most urgent?

Review Questions:

1. What is the goal of the Six Sigma approach to process improvement?
2. How does the Toyota Production System involve employees at all levels in the improvement process?
3. What is the difference between the Lean Six Sigma approach and the Lean Enterprise Institute approach?
4. Can you give an example of an industry where Lean Six Sigma is commonly used?
5. What is the goal of the Lean Startup approach?
6. Can you explain the "stop the line" policy in Toyota plants?
7. How can the Lean approach be applied to front office and back office processes?
8. How does the Lean approach differ from other process improvement methodologies?

Chapter 7:
Phase 1 – Cut the Clutter

Introduction to Phase 1

During Phase 1, primary activities are understanding the Current State of the process and identifying opportunities for improvement. This is achieved through Value Stream Mapping and Process Mapping, which help to identify bottlenecks, delays, and Waste in the process. The goal is to create a clear and detailed map of the current process, so that improvements can be identified and implemented.

When documenting Phase 1, follow these steps:

- Go to Gemba: visit the place where the work is done in order to observe the process in action and identify potential Waste; it may involve time studies, spaghetti mapping, and other tools.

- Identify the inputs and outputs: list the inputs to the process, such as materials, information, and resources, as well as the outputs, such as finished products or services.

- Map the process: create a Flowchart or diagram that illustrates the steps involved in the process, as well as any decisions that are made along the way.

- Identify the problems or challenges: list any problems or challenges that are encountered during the process, such as defects, delays, or bottlenecks.

Going to Gemba

Gemba is a Japanese term that means "the real place." In the context of Lean, it refers to the place where Value is added or where work is done. The idea behind Gemba is that by going to the Gemba, you can see firsthand what is happening and identify opportunities for improvement.

There are several key principles of Gemba:

- **Observation:** By observing what is happening at the Gemba, you can gain a deeper understanding of the work being done and identify problems or opportunities for improvement.

- **Asking questions:** Asking questions and seeking input from those who work at the Gemba can help you better understand their needs and challenges, and identify potential solutions.

- **Respect for people:** Gemba visits should be conducted with respect for the people who work there. This means taking the time to listen to their concerns and ideas, and being open to their suggestions.

- **Continuous improvement:** Gemba visits should not be one-time events, but rather a continuous process of improvement. By regularly visiting the Gemba and gathering feedback, you can identify and address problems before they become serious issues.

To conduct a Gemba visit, you can follow these steps:

1. **Identify the purpose of the visit:** What do you hope to achieve by visiting the Gemba? Are you trying to understand a particular process, identify problems, or gather ideas for improvement?

2. **Plan the visit:** Determine who you will meet with, what you will observe, and what questions you will ask. It can be helpful to create a checklist or Flowchart to guide the visit. Make sure you have permission to visit the work area in the time specified.

3. **Go to the Gemba:** Take the time to observe what is happening and ask questions. Don't be afraid to ask for clarification or additional information.

4. **Gather feedback:** After the visit, take the time to debrief with your team and gather their feedback and ideas for improvement.

When going to Gemba, remember that you're not there to solve problems, change processes, or interrupt the Flow of the work being done. You are using your powers of observation and interviewing techniques judiciously to help inform the Current State Process Mapping, gap analyses, and Root Cause analyses.

SIPOC

A SIPOC is a high-level process map used to quickly visualize a process and its components, providing a clear understanding of what goes into the process, what the process does, and what comes out of the process.

SIPOC stands for Suppliers, Inputs, Process (steps), Outputs, and Customers, which are the headers of the five columns of the diagram. Beneath each column, the specific elements are listed in related rows.

Figure 9: Sample SIPOC

Supplier	Input	Process	Output	Customer
sales team	deal info	design	page mockups	client
client	mockup feedback	refinement	page designs	web developer
client	product info	copywriting	refined page copy	web developer

An example is building a website for a client, where the client is the **Supplier** of the **Input** of information for the site that goes into the copywriting **Process**, which has an **Output** of refined page copy for the **Customer** which is the web developer. Each process step should have one to many rows to identify all the inputs/outputs.

Pro Tip: If a team is struggling to start a SIPOC at the Supplier column, it's sometimes helpful to **jump to the Process column** to list all the process steps in rows. This can come from the Current or Future State Map that is being used, depending on how far along the team is. Once the processes are all listed, work outward to find the Inputs and Suppliers, then Outputs and the Customers.

A robust SIPOC has many rows of information linking each step in the process to the one before and the one after. So the Customer at the end of one row often becomes the Supplier of subsequent rows. The SIPOC diagram is a valuable tool for identifying the inputs and outputs of a process and to highlight areas for improvement, and to **define who should be involved in the process improvement effort (Suppliers and Customers of each Process step).**

SIPOC diagrams are simple, yet powerful, tools that can help organizations identify areas for improvement and streamline processes to increase efficiency and reduce waste.

Takt Time and Cycle Time

Takt time and Cycle Time are two important concepts in the world of Lean manufacturing and process improvement. These concepts are closely related, but they have distinct differences that are important to understand. In this section, we'll define each concept and explore how they are used in the context of Lean manufacturing.

Takt time is a measure of the rate at which a product or service must be produced to meet customer demand. It's calculated by dividing the total available production time by the number of units of product or service that are required to meet customer demand. For example, if a factory operates for 8 hours per day and needs to produce 100 units of product per day, the Takt Time would be 4.8 minutes per unit (8 hours / 100 units = 0.08 hours or 4.8 minutes per unit). This means that a unit of product must be produced every 4.8 minutes in order to meet customer demand.

Figure 10: Takt TIme Equation

$$\text{Takt Time} = \frac{\text{Total Available Time}}{\text{Customer Demand}}$$

Cycle time, on the other hand, is the actual time it takes to produce one unit of product or service. This includes all of the steps involved in the production process, from raw materials to finished product. For example, if it takes a factory 5 minutes to produce one unit of product, the Cycle

Time would be 5 minutes. The goal of Lean manufacturing is to minimize Cycle Time and make it as close as possible to Takt Time. This ensures that customer demand is met in a timely manner and that the production process is as efficient as possible.

Figure 11: Cycle Time Equation

$$\text{Cycle Time} = \frac{\text{Time to complete one unit of work}}{\text{Number of units produced}}$$

At Starbucks, for example, customers order and receive their drinks within a certain timeframe. For example, let's say that during a busy morning rush, Starbucks receives an average of 100 customers per hour. **To meet this demand, Starbucks would need to produce a drink every 36 seconds** (60 minutes in an hour divided by 100 customers). This would be the Takt Time for Starbucks during that specific time period.

Now, let's look at Cycle Time. At Starbucks, the process of making a drink can be broken down into several steps. For example, the customer orders their drink, the barista prepares the drink, and the customer receives the drink. The time it takes to complete each of these steps is the Cycle Time. For example, if it takes a barista 30 seconds to take the order and charge the customer, 60 seconds to prepare a drink, and another 30 seconds for the customer to receive their drink, the **total Cycle Time for one drink would be 120 seconds.**

Knowing both Takt Time and Cycle Time is important for Starbucks to improve efficiency and customer service. If the Cycle Time for making a drink is longer than the Takt Time, it means that the store is not producing drinks fast enough to meet customer demand. This can lead to long wait times and unhappy customers. On the other hand, if the Cycle

Time is shorter than the Takt Time, it means that the store is producing drinks faster than necessary, which can lead to wasted time for employees.

In our simplified example, the Cycle Time of 120 seconds is far greater than the Takt Time of 36 seconds, so Starbucks must allocate more resources to meet demand. In this case, four baristas are needed to produce four drinks about every two minutes, for an average of 30 seconds per drink, which is less than the 36 seconds per drink required to meet demand..

Takt Time and Cycle Time are closely related because they both have an impact on the overall efficiency of the production process.

5S for Success

If the Gemba observations note a lack of 5S and Visual Management, make a separate appointment with the current process owner to either conduct a 5S of the area, or train the process participants to 5S their own areas. 5S and Visual Management are core to "Cut the Clutter" and may improve the area so much that you may need to return later to redo your Gemba observations to find the new baseline for the improvement effort.

Map Out the Current State

Now that you fully understand the Current State, return to the team to discuss your findings. Work together to develop a Current State Map that has consensus from the participants. This should be the nitty-gritty map of all the permutations of the process. This is your "bad" baseline - do not improve, polish, or minimize any of the negative details. Document every instance of Waste and waiting, including:

- Bottlenecks
- Delays
- Excessive work in progress
- Lost information
- Broken communication channels
- Hidden workarounds
- Wandering branches off the happy path
- Steps that generate complaints (especially customer complaints)
- Cost overruns
- Lost income
- Inputs/Outputs (from SIPOC)
- Safety concerns

The easiest Process Mapping is done with sticky notes on a wall, whiteboard, or large paper. It's helpful to have different colors to highlight special notes, and there are some fun shapes out there. However, everyday plain sticky notes will still work just fine. It works best if everyone has a sticky pad and pen to write their ideas.

The Current State Mapping exercise always begins with the official Start and Stop for the process. **What triggers this process beginning and what signifies the end of the process?** Keep in mind that if this process is part of a larger Value Stream, the Start and Stop may be connections to other processes. Avoid the temptation to merge them. Future improvements can be made in those areas later, so keep the scope within the defined process.

After Start, and on the way to Stop, the improvement team should map out every step taken to get from one to the other. **Get into the minutiae here.** It's usually helpful to map out the "happy path" that is the easiest route first. After that's drafted, go back through the whole process to document branches and workarounds (official or unofficial) that exist at each step. **It's important to capture the down and dirty real Current State to be able to fix it later.**

Along the way, be sure to add stickies for Waste, bottlenecks, unnecessary waiting, lost information, broken communication, dead ends, etc. These can be special stickies or a different color ink.

Figure 12: Sample Current State Map

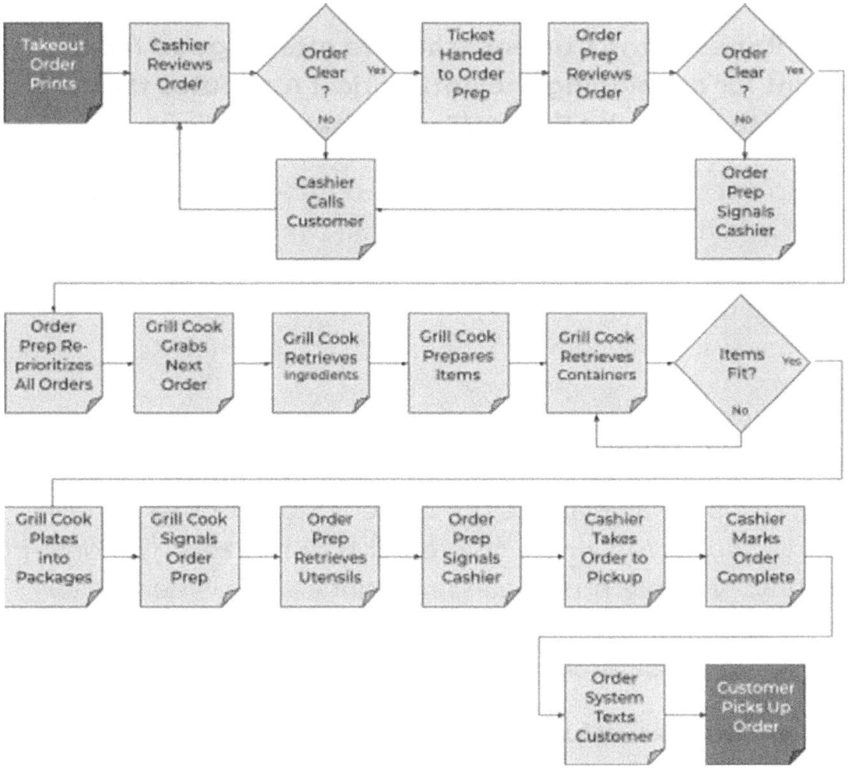

Your Current State Map can also contain an Attributes table that can list tangible measurements of the process and intangible findings such as, "Satisfaction scores below 60%", "22 minutes to get a soggy sandwich", or, "Frustration that feels like bailing neverending bathwater with a slotted spoon while sitting in an overFlowing tub".

One way to categorize Attributes is by True North Metrics of perfection:

- **Quality** - Goal of zero defects
- **Cost** - Goal of 0% Waste, 100% Value
- **Speed/Timeliness** - Goal of 100% on-time, zero delays
- **Human Development** - 100% engaged/satisfied

While perfection is unattainable, the pursuit of perfection is the only way to truly achieve excellence.

Attributes in the Current State are often a good focal point for developing the antithetical Attributes that we want to see in the Future/Target State solutions.

If topics come up that don't relate directly to the mapping exercise, have a parking lot space off to the side where team members can stick notes that need to be addressed later when appropriate.

Value Exercise

Now it's time to evaluate the Current State for the Value in each step. Here's where colored dots or markers will come in handy. Typically, most Lean practitioners use Green, Yellow, and Red dots, but go with what you've got. Each sticker represents a different evaluation of Value:

- **Green = Value Added** (perfect the way it's and where it's in the process, Value-generating from the receiver's perspective and something a customer would pay extra for if it didn't exist)

- **Yellow = Non-Value-Added But Necessary** (the process can't exist without it even though no Value is generated for the receiver)

- **Red = Non-Value-Added** (no Value to the receiver and not required, customers would not pay for this)

Figure 13: Sample Value Exercise on Current State Map

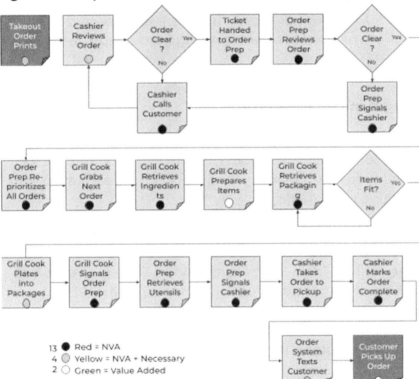

In the example above, there are 13 steps in the process that could be improved or eliminated, only four steps are required to stay the way they are, and only two steps actually contribute Value to the customer. There's a lot of room for improvement!

Here are the keys to doing this Value exercise:

1. **Value is only determined by the receiver**, who is usually a customer of the process. Internal processes can have internal customers, who are typically not the ones working in/with the process.

2. **Assume every step is Red first.** The team has to come to consensus about steps that are upgraded to Yellow (and have the regulating documents handy for review) or Green (and there is consensus that it's what the receiver is seeking from the process).

Magic in the Ideal State

The next step is to produce a Future State Map that represents the to-be process. Before we can start that, we need to get the creativity flowing. And the best way to start is with a little magic.

Before we can truly be open to the possibility of what the ultimate Future State could look like, it can be helpful to start with an Ideal State exercise. Ideal State is a version of the process that exists without constraints, provides immediate Value to the customer in every step, produces zero Waste, and gives fulfillment to everyone involved. **It's the perfect state.** It's the Disney or Star Trek state. It's unbridled magic.

Figure 14: Ideal State

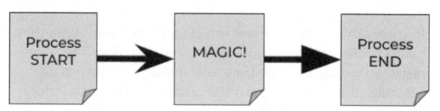

Oftentimes, showing an improvement team an Ideal State Map that looks like this: **"Start → Magic! → End"** is enough to spark some chuckles and some big ideas about what that magic looks like. It's the big ideas that could inspire other ideas for the Future State that may not have been brought up before. Take the big, magic ideas into the Future State Mapping and add the constraints of the real world to scale down to what is possible in the real world.

Go Into the Future (State)

The Future State Map starts with the same Start and End triggers as the Current State so that we can measure the improvement. It's acceptable to carry over any Yellow (Necessary, No Value Added) steps as well as Green (Value Added) steps. Do not carry over any Red (No Value Added) steps unless the Value is improved by reordering the steps or by the positive impact of another step in the process. Here are some examples of each type:

- **Carry over Green steps that are working perfectly.** If the customer gets all the Value they can from it, keep it. Pay attention to any changes in the order and how they impact that Value, though.

- **Carry over Yellow steps that involve actions regulated** by a handbook, policy, rule, or law. While these do not add Value for the customer, it's typically out of the scope of an improvement project to change one of these governing documents. If it can be changed during the period of the improvement effort, add it to the list of solutions (Phase 2).

- Carry over a Red step **if moving it in the process order turns it Green or Yellow.**

- Carry over a Red step **if some other improvement in the process turns it Green or Yellow.**

Sample Future State Map:

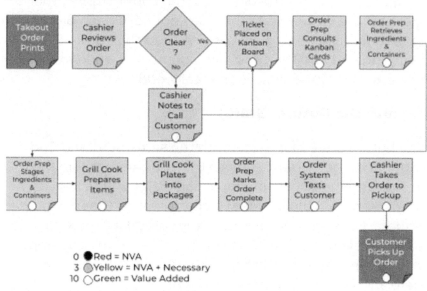

0 ● Red = NVA
3 ◐ Yellow = NVA + Necessary
10 ○ Green = Value Added

In the Future State example above, the team was able to reorganize and refine steps to eliminate Waste and improve Value to the customer. The total number of steps decreased and Non-Value Added steps were converted to Value-Added for the customer.

When completed, the Future State Map should be as close to the Magic State as is possible within the constraints of the project and the organization. Ideally it would reflect only Green and Yellow steps, meaning the maximum amount of Value is getting to the customer.

At the end of Phase 1, you should have a clearer understanding of the process to be improved and the outcomes you hope to achieve by improving it. In Phase 2, we'll use this information to find the causes of the problems in the process, define solutions, and decide which ones to implement. In Phase 3, we'll implement those solutions, measure the results, and set up for continued success.

Chapter 8:
Phase 2 – Fix the Flow

Introduction to Phase 2

In this phase, the focus shifts to implementing improvements to the process. This is done through the use of A3 problem solving, which helps to identify Root Causes and develop effective solutions. The goal is to make incremental improvements to the process, with the aim of eliminating Waste and increasing efficiency.

Plan the Improvements

Based on what you have learned from Phase 1, create a plan for improvement. This might include identifying specific problems of the process to focus on and breaking into sub-teams that collect more data to better understand the Current State or deep dive into specific findings from the Gemba.

Whether the improvement effort is a Kaizen Burst conducted in under a week, or a multi-week project conducted 60 minutes at a time, it's a good idea to develop the plan as a team. Take the time to assign roles, define the deliverables, and establish firm due dates. Doing this will also set a good precedent for Phase 3.

Determine Root Causes of Gaps & Barriers

Analyze the Gaps and Barriers uncovered during the Gemba and Current State Mapping. A Gap is anything missing that prevents reaching the Future State and Barriers are anything that is blocking that path. Document the analysis of the Root Causes of the problems identified. This can be done using tools such as the 5 Whys or fishbone/Ishikawa diagrams.

Risk/Frequency Grid

When trying to decide what issues to focus on next, it may be helpful to facilitate an exercise **using a Risk/Frequency Grid**.

This involves creating a chart with two axiis, with X and Y starting at the bottom-left corner. On the X axis is the Risk (Low to High) and on Y is the Frequency (Low to High). In the middle of the chart create four quadrants and label them High-High (top-right), High-Low (bottom-right), Low-Low (bottom-left), and Low-High (top-left).

Have the team discuss where to place each Gap or Barrier on the grid:

1. **A high-high issue** is detrimental to the process when it occurs and happens with high frequency.

2. **A high-low issue** is detrimental to the process when it occurs but it happens very infrequently.

3. **A low-high issue** causes a minor disturbance to the process and happens with high frequency.

4. **A low-low issue** causes a minor disturbance in the process and happens very infrequently.

Figure 15: Risk/Frequency Grid

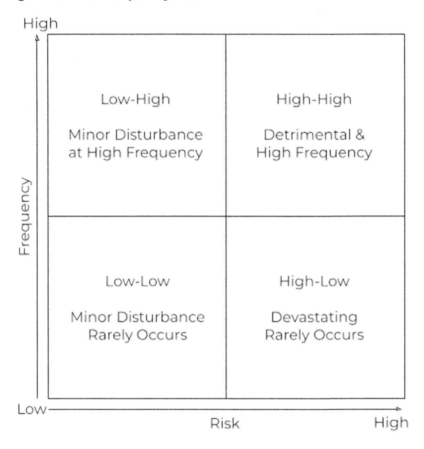

A quick note on team consensus - it doesn't mean that everyone agrees unanimously. Consensus is an agreement from everyone to support the group's decision regardless of their personal choice.

Propose Solution Approaches

Brainstorm individually for ideas to solve the Gaps and Barriers identified. Group brainstorming stifles creativity because some people feel judged when they speak, ideas are scoffed at in the moment, and others feel like they don't have anything important to say. Have everyone on the team brainstorm individually for each Gap/Barrier and return to the team with their list of ideas.

A great tool for sparking new ideas is the 7 Ways method. For each Gap/Barrier, come up with seven unique ways to solve it, at a minimum. Encourage team members to bring all ideas, even if they verge into the Magic State. Sometimes the wild ideas that just aren't possible are still valuable because they might spark an idea in someone else.

Select and Test the Best Solutions

Some Gaps/Barriers may have just one solution that comes up, while others have scores of possibilities. Work together as a team to find the best ones to test. Again, gaining consensus for where to start. The team can always come back to the list if something doesn't work out during testing.

Plan to test solutions in a rapid, controlled way. Small tests of change. Get your lab coat on if it helps get you in the scientific mood, because you're about to experiment.

It should be no surprise that careful planning, caution, and care should be taken. Avoid tests that will cause major disruptions to workFlow or any safety concerns. Often there is little or no funding for testing new solutions, so you'll have to be creative. The goal is to gain a good approximation of the benefit of each choice of solution to determine the best one.

Impact/Effort Grid

A great tool for categorizing the solutions, across all gaps and barriers, is a Impact/Effort Grid. Like the Risk/Frequency diagram, the X axis is for Impact (low to high) and the Y axis is for Effort (low to high).

Figure 16: Impact/Effort Grid

Solutions can be placed in the four quadrants to help decide which to choose, with the following general preference:

1. **High-Low Solution** - High impact with low effort solutions are low-hanging fruit.

2. **High-High Solution** - High impact for high effort solutions may still be worthwhile.

3. **Low-Low Solution** - Low impact for low effort solutions should be considered after 1 and 2, or reserved for the next improvement team to evaluate.

4. **Low-High Solution** - Low impact for a lot of effort solutions is a thankless task.

With solutions brainstormed, tested, and evaluated, it's time to put them into action in Phase 3.

Chapter 9:
Phase 3 – Sustain Your Success

Introduction to Phase 3

In this phase, we'll focus on **institutionalizing the improvements made in the first two phases and ensuring that they are sustained over time**. This phase is crucial in ensuring that the improvements made in previous phases are long-lasting and continue to improve the overall performance of the organization.

Phase 3 includes developing a plan to maintain the improvements made, implementing procedures to ensure that the improvements are sustained over time, continuously monitoring and evaluating the performance of the organization to identify areas of improvement, implementing a plan to make further improvements as needed, and confirming that the improvements made have achieved the desired outcome and are sustained.

Implement the Improvements

Implementing the improvements requires a detailed and well-planned approach. The first step is to create a clear Implementation Plan that outlines the specific actions that need to be taken and assigns responsibility for each action to a specific team member or department. This plan should include a detailed timeline with specific due dates for each action item, as well as a clear communication plan to ensure that all stakeholders are informed and aware of the changes that are taking place.

Additionally, it's important to consider the training and support that will be required for employees to successfully implement the improvements. This includes providing training on new processes, tools, and techniques, as well as providing ongoing support to ensure that employees are comfortable and confident in their ability to execute the changes. Create checklists and guides to assist in maintaining the improvements.

Figure 17: Sample Implementation Plan

#	Description	Assignee	Next Update
1	Communication Plan	DR	Feb 28
2	Print Standard Work	KR	Feb 14
3	Order New Equipment	AH	Mar 15
4	Order Shelving	AH	Mar 15
5	Shelving Installation WO	BB	Apr 01

Considering People Experiencing Change

Change Management is also an important consideration when implementing improvements. This includes identifying potential resistance to change, developing strategies to address resistance, and creating a clear and effective communication plan to ensure that all stakeholders are aware of the changes and the benefits they will bring.

People move through change at their own pace, and helping them move through the change into the new Future State will improve the success of the process improvement. There are several methodologies for Change Management out there, and I really like the Prosci model that bases change on stages of ADKAR (Awareness, Desire, Knowledge, Ability, and Reinforcement). There's specific training to go through to understand how to use ADKAR (and I do not have a license to share that with you), so it's worth checking out what Prosci you can obtain.

Figure 18: Sample Sustainment Plan

#	Description	POC	Date	Planned	Actual
1	Audit Process	DR	Jun 28	>65% on-time	74% on-time
2	Update Standard Work	KR	Jul 14	Jul 14	Jul 18
3	Cost Reduction	AH	Jul 30	5% reduction	3% reduction

Measure and Sustain the Results

It's important to also include a plan for monitoring and measuring the success of the improvements, including identifying key performance indicators and setting targets for performance. This will allow you to track progress and make adjustments as needed to ensure that the improvements are having the desired impact.

Develop a Sustainment Plan to define how to measure the results of the improvements in a structured way. At a minimum, metrics documented in the Current State should be monitored at 30, 60, and 90 days. New metrics may have been defined by the solutions implemented and require monitoring for Sustainment. Finally, the Current State vs Future State attributes tables should be incorporated into the Sustainment Plan.

Confirmed State

To ensure that the improvements are sustained over time, it's important to establish a system for monitoring and measuring progress. This includes setting key performance indicators (KPIs) and targets for performance, and tracking progress against these targets on a regular basis. This will allow you to identify any issues or challenges that may arise and make adjustments as needed to ensure that the improvements are having the desired impact.

Confirm that the desired outcome has been achieved. Evaluate whether the improvements are being sustained over time. Use data and metrics to validate the sustained success.

Additionally, it's important to establish a system for regular communication and reporting on the progress of the improvements. This can be done through regular meetings or huddles with executive leadership, as well as through executive communication to employees and stakeholders. If the problem for the improvement effort came from executive leadership or from a specific daily huddle, begin sharing results in regular reports to that forum. By keeping everyone informed and engaged in the process, it's more likely that the improvements will be sustained over time.

It's also important to conduct regular audits of the process to confirm that the improvements are being sustained. This includes evaluating the process against the original Current State and Future State, as well as against the KPIs and targets that were set. Any discrepancies should be immediately addressed and corrective action taken as necessary.

Finally, it's important to celebrate wins and successes along the way. This helps to build momentum and momentum is the key to Sustainment. When employees see that their efforts are making a difference and that their contributions are Valued, they are more likely to continue to be engaged and committed to the process. By recognizing and rewarding successes, you will create a culture of Continuous Improvement that will support the long-term Sustainment of the improvements.

Chapter 10:
Now Take This Personally

Applying Lean Principles to Your Personal Life

Lean principles can be applied to any process, including those in your personal life. By eliminating Waste and focusing on delivering Value, you can improve the Flow and efficiency of your daily activities and ultimately lead a more fulfilling and productive life.

It Starts With You

The first step in applying Lean to your personal life is to identify your goals. What are you trying to achieve? Whether it's getting fit, organizing your home, or managing your finances, it's important to have a clear understanding of what you're trying to accomplish. Once you have your goals in mind, you can begin to identify the Waste in your current processes.

One of the key principles of Lean is to eliminate Waste. In your personal life, this could mean identifying and eliminating activities that do not add Value to your day. For example, are there certain tasks that you do on a regular basis that do not serve a purpose or that you could outsource to someone else? By eliminating these tasks, you free up more time to focus on activities that are important to you.

Another important principle of Lean is to focus on delivering Value. In your personal life, this means identifying the things that are most important to you and making sure you are dedicating enough time to them. For example, if your family is important to you, make sure you are spending quality time with them. If your health is important to you, make sure you are taking the time to exercise and eat well.

To implement these principles in your personal life, you can start by creating a Value Stream Map of your daily activities.

This is a visual representation of all the tasks you do on a daily basis and how they relate to one another. Once you have identified your Value Stream, you can then begin to identify and eliminate Waste.

I created a 3-page quick-guide for you right after this chapter for you to use to jog your memory when tackling your first challenge.

Grab Your Lean Toolbelt

One of the most powerful tools for eliminating Waste in your personal life is 5S. 5S is a simple and effective method for organizing your environment and eliminating clutter.

The five elements of 5S are Sort, Set in Order, Shine, Standardize, and Sustain. By applying these principles to your home, office, or personal life, you can reduce clutter, improve efficiency, and create a more productive environment.

Another Lean technique you can use is Standard Work, which is a method for documenting and standardizing the best way to perform a task. In your personal life, this could mean creating a morning routine that helps you start your day off on the right foot.

As you're organizing, create a Kanban Board to track all the tasks, goals, and responsibilities you have so you have a visual representation of your progress.

Pro Tip: If your to-do column on your Kanban Board seems overwhelming, try adding a few completed items. Then move the tasks that have been completed along the Kanban board to Done and celebrate. This will start to rewire your mind to see progress over the backlog.

Pillars of Success

By using the same tools and techniques that you have learned in this course, you can improve the way you manage your time, money, and relationships. Here are some examples of how you can apply Lean in your personal life:

- **Time Management:** One of the biggest Wastes in our personal lives is wasting time. We often find ourselves wasting time on activities that do not add Value to our lives or do not bring us closer to our goals. To manage your time more effectively, start by identifying your priorities and goals. Then, use techniques such as time blocking, Kanban boards, and 5S to eliminate time-Wasters and focus on the activities that are most important to you.

- **Money Management:** Many of us struggle with managing our finances. By applying Lean principles to your money management, you can reduce Waste and improve the Flow of your money. For example, you can use Value Stream Mapping to identify areas where you are spending money unnecessarily. You can also use the 5S method to declutter your finances and get rid of unnecessary expenses.

- **Relationships:** Lean principles can also be applied to your relationships. By focusing on delivering Value and eliminating Waste, you can improve the way you communicate with your loved ones and strengthen your relationships. For example, you can use the 5 Whys method to identify the Root Cause of conflicts and misunderstandings. You can also use Standard Work to establish clear communication protocols and ensure that everyone's needs are being met.

- **Personal Development:** Another area where Lean can be applied is in personal development. By focusing on Continuous Improvement, you can set goals for yourself and work towards achieving them. For example, you can use the A3 method to identify areas for improvement and develop a plan to achieve your goals. You can also use Root Cause Analysis to identify the obstacles that are preventing you from achieving your goals and develop strategies to overcome them. If this sounds weird, planning personal conversations, consider how the alternative is working for you now.

Lean is a scientific method to problem-solving, but it doesn't preclude you from personalizing the tools and techniques that work best for you.

Have fun and remember to enjoy your life while you transform it!

In Closing

Through the course of this book, we have covered the key concepts and principles of Lean, including identifying and eliminating Waste, involving employees in Continuous Improvement, delivering customer Value, and using a variety of Lean tools and techniques. We also introduced the 3-Phase Lean approach, which simplifies the elements of a 9-Box A3 and makes it more approachable for everyone.

Whether you are a business leader, an employee, or an individual looking to improve processes at home, the Lean for Everyone mission is to empower you to solve problems and achieve successful results.

It has been my pleasure and realization of a dream to have you holding this book in your hands. I hope that this book has provided you with a solid foundation in the Lean methodology and an approachable set of methods in 3-Phase Lean that you will apply the concepts and tools covered here to improve processes and deliver Value to your customers.

Remember, **Lean is not a one-time event, it's a never-ending journey of Continuous Improvement.** Keep learning, experimenting, and adapting to stay ahead of the curve and achieve success in all aspects of life.

3-Phase Lean Quick Guide

Use this guide to help you successfully solve any problem in your life; at work or at home. This method uses Lean principles in an easy to learn process.

Phase 1: Cut the Clutter
My Current Reality and Goal for the Future

Answer these questions to help document the current state, the pain of staying in the current state, and the target state that would relieve that pain.

1. **What is the problem you are facing?**
   Example: I want to buy a jacuzzi for my backyard

2. **What is the pain you experience in the current reality?**
   Example: I really need to soak my muscles a few nights a week but I'm too tall for my tub. Also, I really have nothing to do in my backyard that relaxes me or is inviting for family and friends.

3. **What does the current state look like, specifically?**
   Example: I do not have a jacuzzi, my bathtub is too small for me to relax, there's nothing for my family and friends to do in the backyard, my concrete patio isn't quite big enough for the jacuzzi I want, there's no utilities near my preferred location for the jacuzzi, and I only have $1000 saved so far.

4. **What does the target state look like, specifically?**

Example: Target state attributes:
- I want to spend no more than $2000 to buy a jacuzzi tub
- Should hold at least 4 adults comfortably
- Placed to the right of the concrete patio where the house can provide privacy from neighbors
- Has a canopy of some kind to keep rain and snow from ruining my hot tub time
- There is a redwood decking surrounding the unit and leading to the patio door

5. **What is the timeframe, realistically?**
Example: I want the jacuzzi, deck, and canopy ready to use by October 1st.

6. **What will happen if this change doesn't occur?**
Example: I will not be able to soak my muscles during ski season and my friends and family will still have nothing to do in the backyard.

3-Phase Lean Quick Guide

Phase 2: Fix the Flow
Things Preventing Me from Obtaining My Target State

1. **What are the gaps between my current state and target state?**
    Examples: Lack of a level area for my jacuzzi, lack of privacy screen, lack of utilities at my preferred location, lack of funds for purchase and installation.

2. **What are the barriers between my current state and target state?**
    Example: I have three family birthdays and a weeklong camping trip that may soak up funds I'd like to save for the jacuzzi.

3. **What are the root causes of the gaps and barriers?**
    Example: Using the 5 Whys method, I found the root cause for my funding issue to be that I never explained my goal to my family. When I did, they supported canceling the camping trip, or scaling it back, to get a little closer to the goal.

4. **What are the solutions to the root causes identified?**
    Examples: Keep a fixed budget for each birthday gift. Scale back or cancel this year's camping trip to save that toward the budget. I also found an electrician who does jacuzzi installations for a flat rate.

5. **Which solutions do I need to test before implementation?**
   Example: Place different shrubbery next to the jacuzzi planned location to determine which is the best height (and return the ones that don't), or whether a trellis with creeping vine would work better.

6. **After testing, which solutions did I decide to implement?**
   Example: Trellis with jasmine vine for screening, which also adds a pleasant aroma to the area.

3-Phase Lean Quick Guide

1. **Make a list of every little thing that needs to be done in order to implement the solutions.**
   Examples: Measure area for jacuzzi, get quotes for deck builder, get quotes for utilities being moved, get brochures and prices for top three jacuzzi choices.

2. **Assign each thing a POC and a specific date for it to be done.**
   Example: Every task has an assigned person responsible for completion and a target date (never TBD).

3. **Track the progress of implementation at each date above and adjust target dates as things change.**
   Example: Progress reviewed at least every two weeks.

4. **Once implemented, recheck for Sustainment on a regular schedule.**
   Example: To get my savings to the $2000 budget, I will need to save at least $150 per week to purchase the jacuzzi at the Labor Day sale.

5. **Throughout this process make notes of insights along the way.**
   Examples:

- What went well? Purchasing and the delivery was smooth.
- What could have gone better? Utilities installation budget went 10% over the $500 budget.
- What are the next steps, if any? Need to put four small bushes and some gravel in the muddy areas on both sides of the deck.

Appendix A: Lean Terms

Here is a list of terms used in Lean, with their definitions:

1. **5S:** A Lean approach to improving organization and efficiency in the workplace, involving Sort (removing unnecessary items), Set in Order (arranging necessary items for efficient use), Shine (cleaning and maintaining the work area), Standardize (establishing and maintaining consistent standards for the first three S's), and Sustain (maintaining the first four S's).

2. **Gemba:** The actual place where work is done, often used to refer to the production floor in a manufacturing setting.

3. **Hoshin Kanri:** A strategic planning and management approach used in Lean, involving the alignment of goals, objectives, and tactics at all levels of an organization.

4. **Kanban:** A Lean approach to inventory control, involving the use of visual signals to indicate when materials or products should be produced or delivered.

5. **Kaizen:** A philosophy of Continuous Improvement, involving small, incremental changes to processes or systems in order to improve efficiency, quality, and effectiveness.

6. **JIT (Just-in-Time):** A Lean approach to inventory management that involves producing or delivering materials or products just in time for them to be used in the production process, rather than producing or stocking large quantities in advance.

7. **Kanban Card:** A physical or electronic card used in a Kanban system to signal the need for materials or products to be produced or delivered.

8. **Kanban Board:** A visual display used in a Kanban system to show the status of materials or products at different stages in the production process.
9. **Kaizen Event:** A structured improvement activity involving a cross-functional team working together to identify and eliminate Waste or improve a process or system over a short period of time (usually 3-5 days).
10. **Lean Six Sigma:** A Continuous Improvement approach that combines Lean principles (focusing on Waste reduction and Flow) with Six Sigma methodology (focusing on data-driven problem-solving and variation reduction).
11. **Lean Startup:** An approach to starting and growing a business that is inspired by Lean principles, and involves using rapid experimentation, customer feedback, and data-driven decision-making to validate business assumptions and achieve rapid growth.
12. **Muda:** Waste or Non-Value-Added activities or processes, as defined in Lean thinking.
13. **Mura:** Unevenness or variability in a process or system, as defined in Lean thinking.
14. **Muri:** Overburden or overwork, as defined in Lean thinking.
15. **Poka-Yoke:** A Lean approach to preventing defects or mistakes, involving the use of simple, foolproof devices or processes to catch errors as they occur.
16. **PDCA (Plan-Do-Check-Act):** A Continuous Improvement cycle used in Lean and Six Sigma, involving the following steps: Plan (define the problem and proposed solution), Do (implement the solution), Check (collect and analyze data to determine the effectiveness of the solution), and Act (implement changes or take other corrective action based on the results).

17. **PDSA (Plan-Do-Study-Act):** A Continuous Improvement cycle similar to PDCA, but with a focus on learning and experimentation.
18. **Root Cause Analysis:** A problem-solving approach used in Lean and Six Sigma to identify the underlying causes of problems or defects in a process or system, rather than just addressing the symptoms.
19. **Single-Minute Exchange of Die (SMED):** A Lean approach to reducing changeover times in a manufacturing setting, involving the identification and elimination of Waste in the changeover process.
20. **Standard Work:** A documented description of the most efficient way to complete a task or process, including the steps, materials, and tools needed to complete the task, as well as the sequence in which they should be used.
21. **Toyota Production System (TPS):** The Lean manufacturing system developed by Toyota, which is characterized by a focus on Continuous Improvement, respect for people, and the elimination of Waste.
22. **Value Stream:** The series of activities required to create and deliver a product or service to a customer, including both Value-adding and Non-Value-adding activities.
23. **Value Stream Mapping:** A Lean tool used to visualize and analyze the Flow of materials and information in a Value Stream, with the goal of identifying opportunities for improvement.
24. **Visual Management:** A Lean approach to communication and problem-solving that involves the use of visual displays and other tools to make information and processes transparent and easily understood by all members of an organization.
25. **Waste:** Non-Value-Added activities or processes, as defined in Lean thinking.

Appendix B: Quiz Yourself

1)What is the main goal of Lean?
a) To minimize Waste
b) To increase efficiency
c) To improve customer satisfaction
d) All of the above
Answer: d) All of the above
> Explanation: Lean aims to minimize Waste, increase efficiency, and improve customer satisfaction by streamlining processes and eliminating unnecessary steps.

2)What is a Lean Kaizen event?
a) A team-based problem-solving process
b) A method for improving efficiency
c) A way to identify and eliminate Waste in a process
d) All of the above
Answer: d) All of the above
> Explanation: A Lean Kaizen event is a team-based problem-solving process that uses a structured method for identifying and eliminating Waste in a process in order to improve efficiency and effectiveness.

3)What is the main goal of the Lean principle "Respect for People"?
a) To minimize Waste
b) To increase efficiency
c) To improve customer satisfaction
d) All of the above
Answer: c) To improve customer satisfaction
> Explanation: The goal of the Lean principle "Respect for People" is to involve and empower employees in the Continuous Improvement process, leading to increased engagement and ultimately improving customer satisfaction.

4)What is the main goal of the Lean principle "Continuous Improvement"?
a) To minimize Waste
b) To increase efficiency
c) To improve customer satisfaction
d) All of the above
Answer: d) All of the above
> Explanation: The goal of the Lean principle "Continuous Improvement"

5) What is the main goal of the Lean principle "Continuous Flow"?

a) To minimize Waste
b) To increase efficiency
c) To improve customer satisfaction
d) All of the above

Answer: b) To increase efficiency

> Explanation: The goal of the Lean principle "Continuous Flow" is to create a smooth, continuous Flow of work in order to eliminate Waste and increase efficiency.

6) What is the main goal of the Lean principle "Pull System"?

a) To minimize Waste
b) To increase efficiency
c) To improve customer satisfaction
d) All of the above

Answer: a) To minimize Waste

> Explanation: The goal of the Lean principle "Pull System" is to minimize Waste by only producing what is needed, when it's needed, and in the quantity needed, using a "Pull" system rather than a "Push" system.

7) What is the main goal of the Lean principle "Standard Work"?

a) To minimize Waste
b) To increase efficiency
c) To improve customer satisfaction
d) All of the above

Answer: b) To increase efficiency

> Explanation: The goal of the Lean principle "Standard Work" is to increase efficiency by establishing clear, standardized processes and procedures that can be followed consistently.

8) What is the main goal of the Lean principle "Visual Management"?

a) To minimize Waste
b) To increase efficiency
c) To improve customer satisfaction
d) All of the above

Answer: b) To increase efficiency

> Explanation: The goal of the Lean principle "Visual Management" is to increase efficiency by using visual aids to clearly communicate information and identify problems in a process.

9) What is the main goal of the Lean principle "Continuous Improvement Culture"?

a) To minimize Waste
b) To increase efficiency
c) To improve customer satisfaction
d) All of the above
Answer: d) All of the above

> Explanation: The goal of the Lean principle "Continuous Improvement Culture" is to create a culture of Continuous Improvement within the organization, leading to the minimization of Waste, increase in efficiency, and improvement in customer satisfaction.

10) What is the main goal of the Lean principle "Just-in-Time"?

a) To minimize Waste
b) To increase efficiency
c) To improve customer satisfaction
d) All of the above
Answer: a) To minimize Waste

> Explanation: The goal of the Lean principle "Just-in-Time" is to minimize Waste by only producing what is needed, when it's needed, and in the quantity needed, using a "Pull" system rather than a "Push" system.

11) What is the main goal of the Lean principle "5S"?

a) To minimize Waste
b) To increase efficiency
c) To improve customer satisfaction
d) All of the above
Answer: b) To increase efficiency

> Explanation: The goal of the Lean principle "5S" is to increase efficiency by implementing a systematic approach to organizing and maintaining a clean, safe, and efficient work environment.

12) What is the main goal of the Lean principle "Gemba"?

a) To minimize Waste
b) To increase efficiency
c) To improve customer satisfaction
d) All of the above
Answer: a) To minimize Waste

> Explanation: The goal of the Lean principle "Gemba" is to minimize Waste by going to the "Gemba" (the actual place where Value is added) to observe and identify opportunities for improvement.

13) What is the main goal of the Lean principle "Kaizen"?

a) To minimize Waste
b) To increase efficiency
c) To improve customer satisfaction
d) All of the above

Answer: d) All of the above

> Explanation: The goal of the Lean principle "Kaizen" is to minimize Waste, increase efficiency, and improve customer satisfaction through Continuous Improvement, involving all employees in the process.

14) What is the main goal of the Lean principle "Value Stream Mapping"?

a) To minimize Waste
b) To increase efficiency
c) To improve customer satisfaction
d) All of the above

Answer: d) All of the above

> Explanation: The goal of the Lean principle "Value Stream Mapping" is to minimize Waste, increase efficiency, and improve customer satisfaction by creating a visual representation of the Flow of work and identifying areas for improvement.

15) What is the main goal of the Lean principle "Root Cause Analysis"?

a) To minimize Waste
b) To increase efficiency
c) To improve customer satisfaction
d) All of the above

Answer: a) To minimize Waste

> Explanation: The goal of the Lean principle "Root Cause Analysis" is to minimize Waste by identifying and addressing the Root Cause of problems rather than just treating the symptoms.

16) What is the main goal of the Lean principle "Poka-Yoke"?

a) To minimize Waste
b) To increase efficiency
c) To improve customer satisfaction
d) All of the above

Answer: a) To minimize Waste

> Explanation: The goal of the Lean principle "Poka-Yoke" is to minimize Waste by implementing simple, foolproof processes that prevent mistakes or defects from occurring.

17)What is the main goal of the Lean principle "Six Sigma"?
a) To minimize Waste
b) To increase efficiency
c) To improve customer satisfaction
d) All of the above
Answer: d) All of the above
> Explanation: The goal of the Lean principle "Six Sigma" is to minimize Waste, increase efficiency, and improve customer satisfaction by identifying and eliminating defects and variability in processes, aiming for a goal of 99.99966% perfection.

18)What is the main goal of the Lean principle "Kanban"?
a) To minimize Waste
b) To increase efficiency
c) To improve customer satisfaction
d) All of the above
Answer: a) To minimize Waste
> Explanation: The goal of the Lean principle "Kanban" is to minimize Waste by using visual signals to control the Flow of work and materials, reducing overproduction and unnecessary inventory.

19)What is the main goal of the Lean principle "Hoshin Kanri"?
a) To minimize Waste
b) To increase efficiency
c) To improve customer satisfaction
d) All of the above
Answer: c) To improve customer satisfaction
> Explanation: The goal of the Lean principle "Hoshin Kanri" is to improve customer satisfaction by setting and aligning strategic goals and tactics, involving all levels of the organization in the planning process, and monitoring progress.

20)What is the main goal of the Lean principle "Muda"?
a) To minimize Waste
b) To increase efficiency
c) To improve customer satisfaction
d) All of the above
Answer: a) To minimize Waste
> Explanation: The goal of the Lean principle "Muda" is to minimize Waste by identifying and eliminating Non-Value adding activities or processes that do not add Value for the customer.

21)What is the main goal of the Lean principle "Muri"?
a) To minimize Waste
b) To increase efficiency
c) To improve customer satisfaction
d) All of the above
Answer: b) To increase efficiency
> Explanation: The goal of the Lean principle "Muri" is to increase efficiency by identifying and eliminating overburden or unnecessary strain on the system, such as overproduction or unnecessary motions.

22)What is the main goal of the Lean principle "Mura"?
a) To minimize Waste
b) To increase efficiency
c) To improve customer satisfaction
d) All of the above
Answer: a) To minimize Waste
> Explanation: The goal of the Lean principle "Mura" is to minimize Waste by identifying and eliminating inconsistency or unevenness in the system, such as variation in demand or capacity.

23)What is the definition for the term Gemba?
a) A place where Value is added
b) A place where Waste is minimized
c) A place where problems are solved
d) All of the above
Answer: a) A place where Value is added
> Explanation: Gemba is a Japanese term that refers to the place where Value is added, such as the production floor or the customer service desk. It's often used in the context of Lean manufacturing to encourage going to the source of a problem or opportunity to observe and understand it firsthand.

24)What is the definition for the term Kanban?
a) A visual signal used to control the Flow of work and materials
b) A system for identifying and eliminating Waste
c) A system for leveling production
d) All of the above
Answer: a) A visual signal used to control the Flow of work and materials
> Explanation: Kanban is a Japanese term that refers to a visual signal used to control the Flow of work and materials in a Lean manufacturing system. It can be in the form of a card, a flag, or an electronic signal, and it's used to signal the need for more materials or to release materials to the next step in the process.

25) What is the definition for the term Muda?
a) Waste
b) Overburden
c) Inconsistency
d) All of the above
Answer: a) Waste

> Explanation: Muda is a Japanese term that refers to Waste or Non-Value adding activities or processes. It's one of the seven deadly Wastes in Lean manufacturing and is used to identify and eliminate activities that do not add Value for the customer.

26) What is the definition for the term Muri?
a) Waste
b) Overburden
c) Inconsistency
d) All of the above
Answer: b) Overburden

1. Explanation: Muri is a Japanese term that refers to overburden or unnecessary strain on the system, such as overproduction or unnecessary motions. It's one of the seven deadly Wastes in Lean manufacturing and is used to identify and eliminate activities that create unnecessary burden on the system.

27) What is the definition for the term Mura?
a) Waste
b) Overburden
c) Inconsistency
d) All of the above
Answer: c) Inconsistency

> Explanation: Mura is a Japanese term that refers to inconsistency or unevenness in the system, such as variation in demand or capacity.

28) What is the definition for the term Takt Time?
a) The rate at which a product must be completed to meet customer demand
b) The rate at which Value is added to a product
c) The rate at which Waste is eliminated from a process
d) All of the above
Answer: a) The rate at which a product must be completed to meet customer demand

> Explanation: Takt Time is calculated by dividing the available production time by the customer demand, and it's used to determine the pace of production and the capacity of the system.

29)What is the definition for the term Single-Item Flow?
a) The practice of producing one product at a time
b) The practice of producing one component at a time
c) The practice of producing one unit of a product at a time
d) All of the above
Answer: c) The practice of producing one unit of a product at a time
          Explanation: One-Piece Flow is a term used in Lean manufacturing to refer to the practice of producing one unit of a product at a time. It's used to eliminate Waste, increase efficiency, and improve quality

30)What is the definition for the term Value-Added Activity?
a) An activity that adds Value to a product or service
b) An activity that does not add Value to a product or service
c) An activity that adds some Value to a product or service
d) None of the above
Answer: a) An activity that adds Value to a product or service
          Explanation: A Value-Added Activity is an activity that adds Value to a product or service from the perspective of the customer. It's an activity that is necessary to create the product or service and that the customer is willing to pay for.

31)What is the definition for the term Non-Value-Added Activity?
a) An activity that adds Value to a product or service
b) An activity that does not add Value to a product or service
c) An activity that adds some Value to a product or service
d) None of the above
Answer: b) An activity that does not add Value to a product or service
          Explanation: A Non-Value-Added Activity is an activity that does not add Value to a product or service from the perspective of the customer

Appendix Z - Edition Changes

2nd Edition:
- Updated copyright
- Leveled white space to help with defining sections
- Added page numbering in footer
- Fixed erroneous auto-capitalization of Lean within words like cLean
- Limited redundant phrasing relating to historical examples of Lean
- Fixed paragraph spacing
- Added bolding to important text
- Normalized capitalization of Lean terms throughout text
- Reformatted section on Employee Involvement to bulleted list
- Edits to Kanban section for clarity
- Edits to Poka-yoke section for clarity
- Separated 5S and Visual Management sections for clarity
- Added a 5 Whys tip
- Added six sigma examples
- Added to LEI and Kaizen descriptions
- Added SIPOC section
- Expanded Starbucks Takt/Cycle Time example
- Expanded Map Out Current State section
- Separated Ideal State from Future State section
- Separated Risk/Frequency Grid section from Root Cause Analysis
- Separated Impact/Effort Grid section from Solution Approach
- Added Change Management section referencing Prosci & ADKAR
- Moved Lean Terms to Appendix A
- Moved Quiz Yourself to Appendix b
- Added 18 illustrations for Lean tools
- Added Appendix Z
- Rasterized PDF to flatten fonts for printing

Made in the USA
Middletown, DE
28 October 2023

41439234R00096